For My Frie[nd]
Taylor — U6M ??

Learn about the magic
of the 1980 # I
Natl Champs —

Good Luck to

Best Wishes [signature]

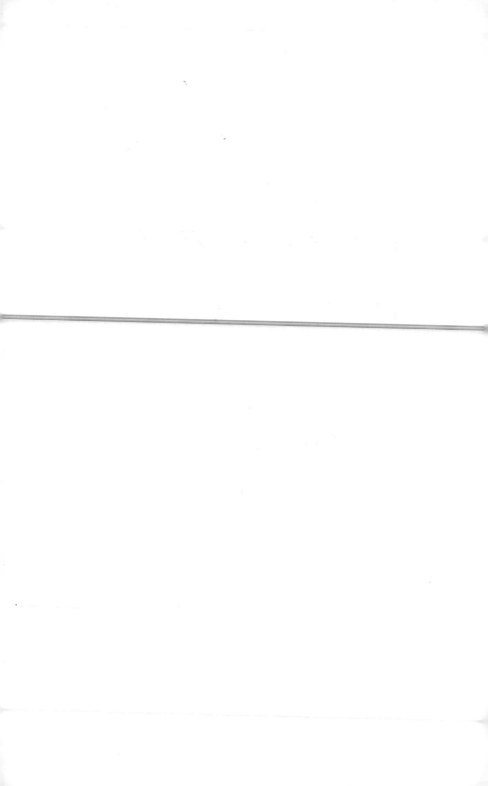

Vince Dooley's

TALES FROM THE
1980 GEORGIA
BULLDOGS

Vince Dooley

with Blake Giles

SPORTS
PUBLISHING
L.L.C.

www.SportsPublishingLLC.com

ISBN: 1-58261-766-X

Publishers: Peter L. Bannon and Joseph J. Bannon Sr.
Senior managing editor: Susan M. Moyer
Acquisitions editor: Mike Pearson
Developmental editor: Elisa Bock Laird
Art director: K. Jeffrey Higgerson
Dust jacket design: Heidi Norsen
Project manager: Kathryn R. Holleman
Imaging: Dustin Hubbart
Photo editor: Erin Linden-Levy
Vice president of sales and marketing: Kevin King
Media and promotions managers: Jonathan Patterson (regional),
        Randy Fouts (national), Maurey Williamson (print)

Printed in the United States of America

Sports Publishing L.L.C.
804 North Neil Street
Champaign, IL 61820

Phone: 1-877-424-2665
Fax: 217-363-2073
www.SportsPublishingLLC.com

This book is dedicated to all members of the 1980 national championship team; not only to the stars, but also to the unsung heroes who sweated on the field and in the weight room, some of whom never got into the game, but all of whom contributed to this wonderful journey.

—V.D.

This book is dedicated to the loyal fans of the Georgia Bulldogs, whose encouragement and support throughout the years was rewarded as never before or since by a special team.

—B.G.

CONTENTS

INTRODUCTION

Georgia won the national championship in football in AD 17. Most calendars reckon the year as 1980, but it was in the 17th year of the reign of Vince Dooley as the University of Georgia's head football coach that the Bulldogs for the first time in their history achieved the pinnacle of success in college football.

Georgia fielded its first football team in 1892 and had enjoyed its share of regional success through its history, winning conference championships in 1920, 1942, 1946, 1948, and 1959. Three times (1927, 1942, and 1946) Georgia had been named national champions on somebody's list but never by the most widely recognized polls.

When Dooley arrived in Athens in December 1963—to a chorus of "Vince who?"—he inherited a program that had been mediocre for most of the 1950s. His predecessor, Johnny Griffith, took three years to win 10 games. Like Griffith, Dooley had been a freshman coach before being hired by Joel Eaves, Georgia's new athletic director as of November 22, 1963, the day President John F. Kennedy was assassinated. What was Eaves thinking?

It was not long before Dooley validated Eaves's choice.

Dooley changed everything, from the uniforms to the staff, at Georgia. And in his third season he won the first of six conference championships. But until 1980, he still had not elevated Georgia to a position among the nation's elite. The Bulldogs were in the national rankings banquet hall, but they rarely sat at the head table and never in the seat reserved for the guest of honor.

As the 1980 season dawned, there was no reason to believe that the upcoming season would be any different. Indeed, the 1970s were a roller-coaster ride for Georgia football fans.

The 1971 team won its first nine games before suffering a devastating 31-20 loss to Auburn, led by Heisman Trophy winner Pat Sullivan and his favorite target, Terry Beasley. That Georgia team finished 11-1 and ranked seventh in the country, but the Auburn loss left a bitter taste to the season. Then the next three years were mediocre, and indeed, the 21-10 loss to Miami, Ohio, in the 1974 Tangerine Bowl was considered the low point of Dooley's career.

From that arose the Cotton Bowl Junkyard Dogs of 1975 and the SEC champs of 1976, who lost soundly 27-3 in the Sugar Bowl to Pittsburgh's national championship team.

Many of the seniors of 1980 arrived in time for Dooley's only losing season in 1977. The Bulldogs played five different quarterbacks that year, running out by season's end. In the final game against Georgia Tech, freshman Scott Woerner was on the sidelines taking snaps in case Davy Sawyer was injured. The problem with that is that Woerner was a punt return specialist who had never taken a snap in a practice at Georgia. Sawyer himself was not expected to play in the varsity game after quarterbacking the freshmen team two days earlier.

The next year was the "Year of the Wonderdogs." Georgia abandoned the Veer Offense, introduced red pants for its road games, and found a tailback in Willie McClendon, who led the Bulldogs to a 9-2-1 record in 1978. The 22-22 tie with Auburn was all that stood between Georgia and a conference title.

But McClendon graduated, and the 1979 team struggled, losing its first three games, the only Dooley-coached team that ever did that. The team never found a tailback. Not to mention, the emergence of sophomore Buck Belue as the starting quarterback ahead of hometown senior Jeff Pyburn created tension.

Would the roller-coaster ride soar again in 1980?

There were more than two-dozen seniors returning, solid players all, but the team was still lacking one piece of the puzzle, that is, until a new kid came to town.

For two years, the state of Georgia had been enthralled with Herschel Walker's apparently superhuman exploits at Johnson County High School in Wrightsville, 100 miles south of Athens. No one had ever heard of a back who combined such speed and size into one package. His high school statistics were obscene. But it was just Class A, the small-school division in Georgia. How would this translate in Division I college football?

The early returns in practice were inconclusive. He sure was fast, and he sure was big, but could he play?

So that was the question as the 1980 season opened for Georgia. What followed was an improbable season that caught the nation by surprise and catapulted Georgia into a position among college football's elite.

And to think it all started with a pig.

—BLAKE GILES

Chapter One

THE PIG

THE STARTING POINT... SORT OF

T he road to the national championship might have started with a discipline problem that took place after spring practice.

The 1980 team became the ultimate team. Every year the staff talked about a point of emphasis, and competing as a team was one of the things we talked about that year. And out of that, coach Erk Russell came up with the "TEAM me" shirts that everyone wore.

"Every new year is new life and a new start," Erk said. "But just point-blank, there was nothing that led me to believe that we were going to win 12 games that season. That's just putting it bluntly. Except we had emphasized team that spring."

Every day we talked about being a team, unselfish play, and "the team wins and everybody benefits." Each coach would get up there on a given day and give his idea of what it meant and talk about it. Putting it all together was how Erk dreamed up those shirts: "TEAM me." Now you see them everywhere.

Erk was always a gimmick guy.

"Yes," Erk said, "every year I would go see Woody Chastain at his sporting goods store with some idea for a t-shirt. I remember he said that it was awful we don't have good enough players to win without all this crap. I saw Woody recently. I reminded him we did the 'TEAM, me' shirts, and if he had been smart enough to trademark those shirts, he would have been a millionaire. Of course, I guess he is a millionaire, but he would have been a multimillionaire."

Tim Morrison, an offensive lineman in 1980, still has his shirt. His 12-year-old son wears it.

So we had really emphasized the team aspect. But there is no doubt that the purloined pig party was a factor in helping the unification of the team.

It started with a tradition the players had, which was called Seagraves. It was a spring tradition they kept to celebrate the end of spring practice.

It was a private party for the team, no coaches allowed. They always drank a lot of beer, but this year they decided to add food to the party. And that proved to be the beginning of trouble for five of our seniors. The whole team participated in the party, but just five of them got caught.

It Seemed Like a Good Idea

I have learned bits and pieces of the story over the years. But I learned pretty quickly the main facts.

First of all, the guilty players were all seniors, cornerback Scott Woerner, rover Chris Welton and linebacker Frank Ros from the defense and two offensive linemen, Nat Hudson and Hugh Nall.

Welton, the man who has the photographic memory, said he doesn't remember who dreamed up the idea.

Ros, our captain in 1980, said he got the idea from the wrestling team.

"I got with Woerner, and we decided we ought to have the best Seagraves ever," Ros explained. "We wanted to do something unique. We didn't have any money to buy food. We had known that the wrestlers had obtained a sow through unorthodox means at the research center. At that age you don't think of any repercussions."

The mastermind?

"You are talking to him," said Woerner, who was an All-America cornerback in 1980. "I knew where we were going to get the pig. I had—what do you call it?—cased the joint a couple of times. I used to go to the Botanical Gardens all the time. It was a neat place for me to hang out, and the hog farm was right next to it. There was a place you could park your car. They had the big hog pens right next to where you could pull up on the road."

"We didn't mean any harm to the people at the swine research center," stated Nall, who was one of the starting centers. "It was just a fun deal that for whatever reason we decided to go that route. We probably could have had any pig farmer in the state of Georgia give us a pig, but once again we were just trying to have the best Seagraves party that had ever been. Prior to that it had always been just beverages with no food. We were going to make sure that we had food provided for our teammates."

Nall ended up being the triggerman.

The perpetrators of the purloined pig were (from upper left to bottom right) cornerback Scott Woerner, rover Chris Welton, captain and linebacker Frank Ros, starting center and triggerman Hugh Nall, and offensive lineman and barbeque chef Nat Hudson.

"I was the one with the bow and arrow," he said. "I'm an avid outdoorsman. I had done it since high school, but only a little bit since I had been in college."

"Hugh didn't take much convincing," Woerner added with a laugh.

Hudson, a big offensive lineman, was recruited because he had some experience barbecuing hogs. Defensive end Pat McShea might have been in on the caper except that he was out with his girlfriend. Offensive guard Tim Morrison was invited, but he chose to stay home with his wife.

The Procuring

The UGA farm is just a short drive, less than three miles, from the athletic dorm. So it was a quick trip for the live Bulldogs late that night to the pigpens.

Woerner held his flashlight while Nall took aim. Hudson was standing by with a blanket.

"When you are shooting something in a 100-foot pen, it is not like you have to wait for it to come by," Woerner said.

Nall hit the pig with his first shot, but it was not fatal.

"The first time he shot him, he hit him a little too far back," Woerner remembered, "and he was running down that hog wire fence. The arrow sounded like somebody put baseball cards between the spokes of a bicycle."

"The first one hit him in the shoulder blade and didn't go into him," Nall echoed. "The pig turned and walked—I can hear him right now—and walked down the fence, and the arrow sounded like those old baseball cards you used to put in the spokes of your bicycle. He was trying to get away from us.

"Hudson was there with a blanket ready to jump on him. I got around to make my second shot, and I angled it in behind the shoulder blade. It was a good hit, and I saw it penetrate, and the pig jumped, it looked like 10 feet in the air. It hit the ground, and Hudson was on top of him with that blanket to keep him from squealing. I think he had done that kind of thing before."

"He jumped straight up," Woerner confirmed. "I never thought a 400-pound hog could jump up in the air like that. It was pretty amazing."

The pig proved more adept at self-elevation than the five players did at lifting him over the fence.

"Have you ever tried to pick up a 400-pound sow?" Woerner asked. "We couldn't get it over the fence."

"The sow was huge," Ros recalled. "The five of us couldn't pick the thing up. We were strong, but we had to gut the thing in the field to get it out. That was comical."

"I don't think we did the best selection," Nall opined. "The smaller one would have been better. Once she was down, we couldn't move her. It was supposed to be one of those things where we picked her up and threw her in the back of the car. We had to field dress the pig right there to lighten the load, and once we got her to the fence, we had to prop her on the fence."

"We leaned it up against the fence and flipped it over," Woerner explained.

"It was a real stout fence," Nall added.

A CLOSE CALL

The getaway vehicle was an Oldsmobile Toronado. The slain hog was finally hoisted into the trunk for transport to Poss's Lakeview, a banquet facility owned by Bob Poss, a Bulldog letterman from the early 1940s, who had the concession contract at Georgia football games and owned a catering business.

On the way to Poss's, however, the players stopped at a gas station.

"We pulled in for some gas," Ros recalled. "Here are four white guys and a big black guy, and he had a cook's outfit on. He was muddy from trying to get the pig out. He was covered in mud and blood. We had a tarp on the pig, but the tarp blew over just as a cop was coming down Baxter. He did not stop. I never figured that out."

Defensive end Robert Miles remembered Hudson, his roommate, coming back to the room, covered in blood.

"What happened?" Miles asked.

"Hog blood," Hudson replied succinctly. "Hog blood."

THE COOKING

Hudson barbecued the pig that night using a chain-link fence gate as a grill.

"Nat knew how to do it because he grew up doing it," Ros said. "He cooked it all night."

"I think Nat had something he was swabbing on the pig," Nall added. "I know he had a big stick with a rag on the end of it. He was the head cook."

Woerner pronounced the party a grand success.

"There were 127 cases of beer and eight kegs," he said. "We had about 20 or 25 cases left, and when we had to hang around later that spring, it got us through."

What went on at the party was standard fraternity fare. The upperclassmen mounted the head on a stick and made freshmen kiss its snout.

CAUGHT!

The whole episode might have gone undetected except for some careless actions by some of those freshmen.

"The older guys went back to the dorm," Welton said, "and the freshmen who had been initiated got the bright idea to cut the head down. They threw it in the back of a truck, and they went driving around campus and dumped it on the steps of one of the high-rise dorms."

What happened out there among the team normally always stayed with the team. But then a couple of them made it public. There were a couple of students smooching, and they dropped the carcass at the couple's feet. It scared the girl to death, but the boy got the license number of the player's truck.

THE FALLOUT

Mitch Mullis, a walk-on from Athens who had just recently earned a scholarship on the field, was the driver. Originally he was one kid who got in trouble because it was his truck. But that bothered Ros.

"He didn't steal the pig. I went to Scott and said, 'It is not right,'" he confessed.

Woerner was watching the NCAA tennis tournament on our campus when Ros found him with the news that Mullis had been caught.

"You have got to turn yourself in," Ros told him.

Woerner said he didn't see any reason to do that, but it didn't really matter because I already had his name.

I don't remember exactly how I found out about it, but I do remember calling the faculty member who was in charge. The pig was his responsibility. I was trying to tell him how upset I was and that I assured him that it would be repaid and that I would discipline the players.

And then I remember making a statement that as soon as I made it, I knew I had said the wrong thing. I told him, "I know this will be hard to believe, but these are five of the finest individuals I have on the team." And followed that with, "Well, I know what you are going to say, I must be in a hell of a shape if these are five of the finest individuals."

But they really were. Welton is so well-respected today. Nall and Hudson from the offensive line. Ros, Woerner. You had a pretty good group of people.

But I quickly caught myself, and I told him, "Let me assure you, that if you will let me handle this, these young men will learn their lesson."

A LESSON IN LEADERSHIP

Frank Ros said he learned lessons in leadership from both Erk Russell and me. And he said the way I handled the pig incident taught him a few things.

"He was ticked," Ros said. "He called us in, and you could tell he was angry. He was shocked.

"But I learned not to make an emotional decision. That is something to this day that I still do. You may be mad and you may be angry. Sleep on it for 24 hours and get the emotions out.

"He told us he was going to get to the bottom of this thing. In the meantime, we had to stay in the dorms. This was spring. Prime time. We sat in our rooms for two weeks."

The first meeting I had with them, when I called them into my office, I just laid into them about how embarrassing this was. I told them I was so mad that I didn't even want to talk to them so I confined them to their rooms for a couple of days. They couldn't leave except to go to class.

Then a few days later they came back, and I told them what the punishment would be. I took them off scholarship. To earn their keep, they had to work, and part of that work was to paint the wall around the practice field during the hottest part of the day.

And I tried to scare them.

"Well, my first reaction is to just kick you all off the team," I said. "Besides, let me tell you how serious this is. These are experimental pigs that were injected with various types of serum. This particular one could be the one they were concerned about that might make you impotent."

I don't think all of them knew what that meant, but most of them did. I let them think about that for a few days. I put them through some hell, but they deserved it.

"Hugh and I walked out of there kind of chuckling," said Woerner, who I found out did not put much stock in the comment about possible impotence.

Welton said that the scariest thing for him was that look that I gave them in my office.

"I remember that look," he said. "Looking us up and down. That stare was the worst thing.

"The story I like to tell is this: I look around and next to me is Hugh Nall, our starting center, and Frank Ros, our team captain, Nat Hudson, All-SEC guard, and Scott Woerner, All-America cornerback, and I think we dodged that bullet. I'm thinking, 'What are you really going to do, Coach?' We had our scholarships taken away for the summer, and we had to work and paint that wall. So I learned that if you are going to do something bad, do it with guys who are pretty good."

Ros remembered it vividly.

"He calls us back in there. 'I've got a good mind to throw you all off the team.' In the end he told us, 'You all have to stay in summer school, you all have to attend classes, and you have to live in university housing and eat university food. You will work to pay restitution, and you will work out with coach [John] Kasay.'

"The job was working with the athletic groundskeepers at first, working at the stadium. Then they decided to have us paint the walls on the perimeter of the practice field. Each field was 120 yards, the grass field and the Astroturf. We had to paint it all summer long. The 1980 summer is still the record hot summer. There were 22 days it was over 100 degrees. You can look it up."

"It was the hottest summer on record," Woerner agreed.

"We would go to class and after lunch work from 1 p.m. to 4 p.m. painting the wall and then work out with Coach Kasay and then go to night class," Ros said. "We did that the whole summer. Paint that cinderblock wall. It was hot and miserable. We got about 10 to 15 yards from the end. It was hotter than hell. In comes Coach Dooley in his Lincoln Town Car."

It sounds like a scene out of a grade B movie, a sinister fellow hidden behind a tinted window, revealed slowly as the electric window descends.

"He looks at us," Ros recalled, "and says, 'It ain't good enough. Do it again.' Here we go, just as we get to the end and start all over. Every bit of money we made, we never saw it; it went straight to restitution."

The five seniors spent countless hours together that summer, talking about the things that all young men talk about.

"We were trying to avoid Kasay," Woerner said. "We didn't have any place to hide. We didn't have any money."

Ros admitted that he violated one condition of his sentence.

"Welton, Nall, and I got an apartment at Sussex," he said. "We had our room at the dorm, but we had residents looking out for us."

Welton's parents almost couldn't believe that he had been involved in this incident. He was in many ways the "fair-haired child."

(Welton turned out to be a well-respected professional in sports marketing. He went to law school. He was with King and Spalding, one of the best law firms in the state. Then he worked with Billy Payne for the Olympics. Through that association he formed his own company to be the advertising agent for all of the Olympics. He sold that about the time I retired.

There were some who pushed Welton to be my successor as athletic director, and the search committee talked to him. He could have been a good one.)

David Davidson of the Atlanta paper broke the pig story first, getting a lot of his information from backup quarterback John Lastinger. I think he kind of led Lastinger on that he knew more than he did.

"Somebody tricked him pretty good," Ros laughed. "Of course, it is not that hard to trick a freshman. It got in the paper, and then in *Sports Illustrated* after that."

Needless to say, I was not too pleased with any of this.

A RALLYING POINT

When defensive coordinator Erk Russell looks back to the seeds of greatness for the 1980 team, he starts where many others start with the quality of people on the team.

"We had some good people, and the attitude was good," he said, "but damn if I don't believe we built on the hog story."

There were many others who believed that the "purloined pig," as the headlines in the Atlanta newspaper called it, was a catalyst for team unity that could not have been manufactured.

"I wouldn't attribute our success to that incident," Chris Welton said, "but it was one of the factors. The five of us were all going to stay in the summer anyway. By having to work, a lot of the younger guys thought we had stepped up and taken responsibility."

"The five of us, we were the team leaders," Scott Woerner recalled. "We came back in the best shape of anybody on the team.

It brought a lot of people together, mainly us. Everybody was close."

"I remember when Coach Russell was in the dining hall right after we got caught," Welton pointed out, "and he said, 'Chris, come over and eat with me.'

"And he said, 'Well, I understand we stole a pig.'

"'Yes sir, we did.'

"The fact he used the term we stuck in my mind. We got in trouble, but everybody felt a part of the incident. Everybody felt responsible, but we took the fall. That caused people to appreciate us a little more, being responsible for what we did. That probably did have some carryover."

Erk knew I was tough on them for good reason.

"The rest of the team knew the origin of the pig and what happened," Erk said, "Hugh and Frank, all of them, were in positions of leadership on the team, and darn it I don't think it was a bond for everything.

"Now that may seem far-fetched to you, but it doesn't to me. Right off the bat, they had something in common. It drew the people together and the team, too."

"It brought the team together," Frank Ros said. "Coach Russell said he was glad it happened."

This summertime crisis could well have been part of the glue that brought this team together, perhaps more so than any team that I coached during my 25 years.

Chapter Two

THE STAFF

PUTTING TOGETHER A STAFF

I've always felt that it was important to have a staff with a balance of about two-thirds to one-third. By that I mean I wanted two-thirds inbred and loyal to the program, but I did not want to get so stagnant and so inbred that we did not have new ideas coming in and new ways of doing things.

That 1980 staff was a perfect example with George Haffner and Bill Lewis coming in that year. They were able to give new life and infuse some new thoughts without disturbing the foundation that we had built. They were the type of people who had an appreciation for the tradition, for the foundation.

So they brought in some ideas, but they were not radical. They understood that we had a winner here. Their attitude was, "Let's see if we can make it better," as opposed to saying, "This is not the way I am used to doing it."

They were such good people, too, and that is important, that you hire those kinds of people to begin with. The technical knowledge came later.

George came in as the new offensive coordinator, replacing Bill Pace, who had gone to a similar position at Tennessee. Bill Lewis was our new secondary coach, replacing Jim Pyburn.

There was a lot of controversy the previous year involving Jim's son, Jeff, who was competing with Buck Belue at quarterback. Pyburn was a senior who had started, but he eventually lost the starting job to Belue. That certainly had an effect on Jim. It was so hard on Jim and Ann, his wife.

Bill had worked with Frank Broyles, and Frank had recommended him highly. In fact, Bill Pace had also worked with Broyles, and he was the connection that helped bring Bill Lewis to Georgia. He was absolutely as detailed as any coach I ever had. He just insisted on it. He was demanding, and he wanted it done. He was immaculate in his appearance, too. That was the way he was. He was a contrast to Erk Russell. They blended well.

George was a likeable guy. He was Chicago. That was where he was from, and at times his accent would come out, and we would kid him about that. He fit in well. He stressed the fundamentals. He was a competitor.

The holdovers on the staff included Erk, our defensive coordinator and defensive line coach; Steve Greer, who coached defensive ends and was also our recruiting coordinator; and Chip Wisdom, our linebackers coach. Steve and Chip had both played for me at Georgia.

Our offensive staff included three other former players: Charlie Whittemore coaching the receivers and Mike Cavan coaching the backfield, while John Kasay was an assistant line coach and oversaw our conditioning program. Wayne McDuffie was the head offensive line coach. Rusty Russell, Erk's son and another Georgia letterman, was a graduate assistant. Bill Hartman was our volunteer coach, and he handled the kickers, and Doc Ayers had administrative duties.

Obviously, everybody had a position to coach, but in addition, they had a responsibility to the kicking game. For example, Bill was in charge of punt returns, which would have been logical because he coached the secondary and they would be on the field. George would have had the punt teams, because that would have fit in with the offense. Everybody worked together, but that one person was in charge of that specific area. He had to get everybody organized.

A New Face

The first newcomer to the staff in 1980 was Bill Lewis, who the previous year had been the head coach at Wyoming.

Bill Pace was still on our staff at the time. He and Bill Lewis had made a connection at Arkansas and had gotten to know each other. When Jim Pyburn decided to retire, Bill Pace was the one who recommended Bill to me.

After his interview, I offered Bill the job on New Year's morning. The American Football Coaches convention was that week, but he wanted to come into Athens and get settled and learn the players, so that he was ready to be productive.

Bill traveled to Athens and checked into the Ramada, and it was not 15 minutes before he got a call from Pace telling him that he had accepted a position at Tennessee. One of the reasons he had

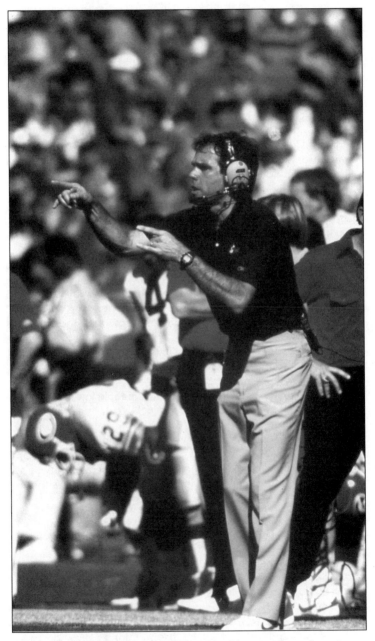

Bill Lewis was nicknamed "Mad Dog" by his secondary players.

taken the job in the first place was to work with Pace, and here Pace was leaving.

"He came by the hotel and assured me that he was not leaving because there was anything wrong with the Georgia program," Bill recalled.

While the rest of the staff was at the convention, Bill spent a few days reviewing game films from 1979, learning the system and the players. As soon as the staff returned, Bill went straight into a meeting with Erk Russell.

"I asked for a copy of his defensive playbook," Bill said. "I thought I was getting a feeling of how they did things from the films, but they were flip-flopping a lot of guys, so I wanted to see the playbook."

"We don't have a defensive playbook. It's all up here," Erk told him, pointing to his bald head.

Erk felt more secure in not scattering defensive schemes all over the landscape.

"That way I don't have to worry about things leaving here," he told Bill.

"That was a unique introduction to what Erk was all about," Bill said. "He offered to sit down with me to review any questions I had. As I found out later, it was amazing how well those players knew and played that defense."

Bill helped some with recruiting in his first days on the staff, but the bulk of his time was spent familiarizing himself with the secondary.

"What I quickly learned was that those people knew a lot more about the defense than I did," he said. "I truly mean that. They coached me up on it.

"What was so impressive was their knowledge of what they were doing. A player came in as a freshman and learned that Split 60 and all the nuances, and when he left as a senior, he was still playing exactly the same defense. Jeff Hipp and Chris Welton and Greg Bell—they knew that defense inside and out."

"MAD DOG" JOINS THE STAFF

The players themselves tell a slightly different version of the story. Jim Pyburn had been their secondary coach only one year, but it had been a difficult year.

"[Pyburn] wasn't teaching us anything," explained Greg Bell, a senior cornerback in 1980. "I can't tell my children, 'You did something wrong,' and just scream. He had nothing to draw on to say,

'This is how you do it.' In came Bill Lewis, and he was very detailed. He was on us like a duck on a June bug if we took one step wrong. We came up with a nickname, 'Mad Dog.' It wasn't that he was yelling or screaming. He was like a mad dog, vicious, and he wouldn't let go."

Senior defensive back Bob Kelly actually coined that nickname, which stuck with Bill as long as he was at Georgia.

"That was what our coach called one of our players at Furman," Kelly recalled. "He had a raspy voice, like when Coach Lewis lost his voice after the first day of practice. They both were way more intense than a normal mental person would be."

At first, "Mad Dog" was a secret name for Coach Lewis, used only behind his back. But eventually, the players revealed the nickname, and he embraced it with good humor.

"Bill was by far the smartest, best technical coach that I was ever around," Kelly praised. "He knew what all 22 guys were doing on every play."

"He was a great person to explain the whole scheme of the defense," cornerback Mike Fisher agreed. "He could go down the line and explain offensive blocking schemes and possibly how somebody was going to release. If you could look at the detail he would put forth on offensive plays and defensive schemes and tendencies, it was very, very in depth, and very complete. You went over it day in and day out from Sunday afternoon to Saturday at game time."

"Bill Lewis got the most out of us four or five white boys that anybody could get," Bell said. "We played over our heads."

FRESH THINKING ON OFFENSE

Wayne McDuffie, our line coach, was the one who recommended George Haffner. He had a pretty good background, and when I interviewed him, I thought he was solid. Philosophically, he fit in, but he would also bring expansion to the passing game. I wanted someone to expand the passing game, but yet not to the extent that we would lose the base of what we had established.

He had an appreciation for being a sound football team, for not making mistakes. That fit into my philosophy very, very well. That was so fundamental to what we did, which was first of all not to beat yourself. So we wanted to keep that. George was able to fit that bill, and he was the right type of person—loyal—a company man, so to speak.

We had run the Veer Formation in the mid-1970s, but after we led the nation in turnovers in 1977, we went back to the I Formation, and George was very familiar with that attack. Indeed, it was one reason he had gone to Texas A&M in the first place.

You could make a case that our offense had hundreds of plays, but sometimes that was because there was a base play with a lot of different sets. That gave you some flexibility and different ways to get into a play. There was always the danger with so many plays that you didn't do any of them well. We tried to have the base plays and do them well.

We didn't make a lot of changes at the line like you see now. We had hot receivers and hot reads. We had sight adjustments based on the alignment of the defense, but it was not nearly as elaborate as you see now.

People ask me, "What is the difference between today and yesterday in football?" The one difference, the only difference, is the sophistication of the passing game. Everything else is the same. You have got to run the football. You have to block on the offensive line. You will always have the fundamentals of blocking and tackling.

Of course, we did not have Herschel Walker during George's first spring. We were trying to establish and get a sound offense with more balance. Of course once the season started, it became more and more an emphasis of getting the ball to Walker in different ways. He proved to be the one missing link. Everything else was there: the offensive line, the quarterback, a kicking game, and a solid all-around football team.

IMPRESSED RIGHT AWAY

George Haffner and I had met each other, but we were not friends before he came to the staff. George was on the staff at Pittsburgh when we played them in 1973 and 1975 under Johnny Majors. I also knew he had coached under Bobby Bowden at Florida State.

He was at Texas A&M when I called, and he was immediately interested.

"I liked the area from my time at Florida State. I was very interested in the stability of the program," George said. "Florida had called me about 10 days before. Charlie Pell was their new coach. But I didn't know him, and I just didn't think it was the right situation."

One of George's first assigned goals was to develop a program to work with quarterback Buck Belue.

"Buck needed a little personal training," George recognized. "He was playing baseball that spring, but I was able to work with him some, and I got a chance to see how he could handle different situations. Football was important to him. I could see that by how he worked and how he competed."

TOUGH GUY TO PLAY FOR

Although he was not new to our staff in 1980, line coach Wayne McDuffie fit into that one-third of coaches brought up in other programs. He joined us in 1977.

Football was his life. He was a real competitor. He was a tremendous help to our staff. He was a good recruiter. He knew what it took to be good at it. He was totally committed to success in recruiting, too. He studied it, and he knew what kind of athletes to recruit.

But he couldn't turn it off. It was not commonly known, but I understood that he had been diagnosed with bipolar disorder for which he took medication.

He worked the team hard. They responded and were well conditioned. But sometimes after Wednesday's practice, we would tell Wayne to take off and go recruiting. Thursday and Friday was when you want to bring the team back, and he was always so uptight after working with them on Monday, Tuesday, and Wednesday that he was better off to go recruiting on Thursday and Friday. The players welcomed that break.

"We would look at the gate and hope he would not come through," center Joe Happe admitted. "He was a tough, tough guy to play for. It became a badge of honor to play for him."

"He was always challenging you," tackle Jeff Harper said. "He kept a space between us and him, a fear factor. You always knew who was the boss. He wasn't your friend. You could never let your guard down around him."

Like many competitive athletes, Harper accepted playing under Wayne as a challenge.

"I wanted to prove to myself and to him that I belonged," Harper said. "I think the whole offensive line took on his personality in 1980. We had developed cohesiveness among ourselves. We took pride in whatever he dished out, that it was not enough."

"God rest his soul, he was a very demanding coach," guard Jim Blakewood agreed. "I can't imagine there being a tougher coach. It really gave us an edge. We felt like nobody in the league worked harder than we did. The teams we were getting ready to play couldn't survive our practices. The games were a piece of cake. He was very demanding, but he knew his stuff."

"He was one of the toughest guys in the world to play for because of the commitment he required," guard Tim Morrison said, "until you understood that he was trying to make you better than you ever thought you could be. We clashed a lot, but I had respect for him, because I was raised that way. He and I became close friends after my playing days were over."

"Practice was tough, intense," Happe added. "The game was a piece of cake. It was motivation through fear. But there were times he would surprise the heck out of you. One of those times he came into the film room and he told me to get up out of my chair. 'You can sit in my chair because of the game you played. I want to recognize you for the game you played.'"

Happe reminded me how Wayne's intensity got him in trouble with me. We wanted the players to be finished with all football meetings and practice by the time they ate dinner. That gave them some time to focus on their studies or have some down time.

"He used to sneak us up to watch film in the old wrestling room on the fourth floor of the Coliseum," Happe relayed. "While we were eating dinner, he would come by and say, 'Meet me on the fourth floor in an hour.' We would go and watch film for another hour and go through plays."

That was until I came through and caught him.

"He sent us home and chewed out Coach McDuffie," Happe confessed.

BAD COACH, GOOD COACH

John Kasay came to Georgia as a player before I was hired. The previous staff recruited him, though by the time he was eligible for the varsity, I was the head coach.

We were tough on that first team, tough but fair.

"It was immediately apparent from day one," John agreed. "I remember my roommate, Frank Lankewicz, and I were lying in bed, wondering, 'Vince who?' Someone told me he had been the freshman coach at Auburn, and I remembered the Auburn freshman team hit hard.

"The first meeting we had was at 3 p.m. in old Stegeman Hall. I was there early. Bill Dooley, his brother, walked in. He was the enforcer on the staff, the sheriff. He had come to Athens from Mississippi State, but he would have done anything to get out of Starkville.

"That first meeting, all he did was lock the doors at 3 p.m. and then take role call."

Everybody who was late had extra conditioning.

"I figured out real quick that they were going to straighten it out from the ground up," John said.

We wanted to see who was going to commit to us and who wasn't.

As a coach, John was the guy who had to massage egos after they were bruised by Wayne McDuffie.

"Coach McDuffie was the bad guy and Coach Kasay the good guy," Tim Morrison posited. "A lot of guys thought about transferring."

Morrison admitted that he even considered it, and circumstances gave him the opportunity after his freshman year. Small colleges were recruiting his brother, Paul. Their father had recently had back surgery, so Morrison went with his brother on some of his recruiting trips.

They would look at Morrison and say, "Oh, we want you to transfer."

"There were a lot of times I thought I could be the big fish in the little pond," Morrison admitted. "But I really do appreciate the opportunity to play for Wayne at Georgia."

"There was no middle ground with Wayne," John recalled. "He couldn't waver. He was ultra-critical. He wanted it to be perfect. When Jimmy Vickers was here, I was the bad guy. When Wayne was here, I was the good guy."

John was as close to Wayne as any of our coaches, so he knew him very well. He called him "a misunderstood guy."

They became good friends over time, but Wayne did not trust John at first. John spent a lot of time with our players. They may not have liked him, but they respected him.

"I had the confidence of every one of these players," Kasay said.

"Coach Kasay should have been a comedian," Jim Blakewood said. "He would keep things light. He had funny stories to tell. I always enjoyed being around him."

John had by design a split personality. Aside from assisting Wayne with the offensive line, he played two other significant roles. He and Sam Mrvos ran the offseason conditioning program, and John and his family lived in the athletic dorm, where he could keep an eye on things.

"I felt I had an instinct for conditioning athletes," John said. "I considered myself a good horse trainer. A horse trainer goes out there with an idea of what he wants to do, but while he is watching that horse, he sees something and he adjusts his mind according to what he sees that day. If that horse is laboring, he knows he may hurt him. I had that sense. I knew when to press the button and when to make them angry. It was in the plan."

He paid close attention to the effort and to the results. The athletes might be working smoothly, but they might hit a plateau, which meant they needed encouragement to reach for a higher level.

"You cannot stay on a plateau long or else you will go down," John stated. "I would go out there and be supercritical. Before long they were angry. Then I get angry back, and before you know it we are working like crazy. I am more involved, and they are more involved. I still get letters from guys: 'Keep them pissed off.' They realized that when they were angry they got more out of themselves."

FOUR WHO PLAYED FOR ME

Mike Cavan, Steve Greer, Charles Whittemore, and Chip Wisdom were the young lions on the coaching staff. They had played for me, and were youthful and totally committed to Georgia. Their hearts were not only committed to Georgia: They *were* Georgia.

Mike was our quarterback on the great 1968 team. His dad had been a football coach, so he knew the game. Plus, he had the personality that he could walk into a room and light it up. He is jovial, and people respond to him. That was one reason he was able to lead a veteran team like we had in 1968 with veterans like Bill Stanfill, Jake Scott, and Brad Johnson.

Mike was easy to like, and it was helpful to him in recruiting.

On the sidelines Mike was Mr. Enthusiasm Extraordinaire. When the players on offense came off, he would run out to greet them and jump up and down with them.

Charlie Whittemore was a receiver for us in the late 1960s. He had been at Vanderbilt for some time. Charlie was loyal, dedicated, committed, a Georgian through and through.

Our linebacker coach was Chip Wisdom. He was bright and very competitive. He was on that 1971 team that did so well. He was a very good linebacker. He was tough and a good recruiter. And he could talk. It was a good asset. Chip was also very enthusiastic.

The other ex-player was Steve Greer, who coached our defensive ends and was our recruiting coordinator. He was a small defensive lineman, but he was quick, relentless, and tough enough to earn

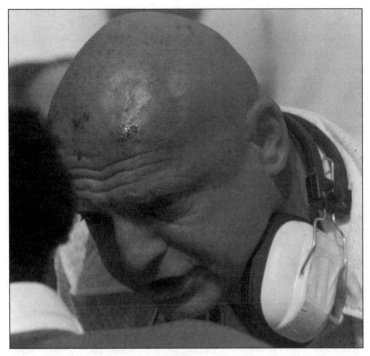

Defensive coordinator Erk Russell got the most out of his players.
Note the blood on his forehead from his pregame ritual of head-
butting with his players.

All-America recognition in 1969. Steve was not as outwardly
enthusiastic, but there was never a greater competitor as a player.

ERK

The first person I hired when I came to Georgia was Doc Ayers,
and the second was my brother, Bill. So Erk Russell was not the first
person I hired, but he was on the first staff. We didn't know it, but
1980 was our last year together, so we were together for a long
time.

The first time I remember meeting Erk was while he was coaching at Grady High School. He was visiting Auburn and was sitting in
my apartment, and my first impressions were that he was a gregar-
ious person. You couldn't help but notice his bald head. He had a

can of beer and a cigar and appeared to be thoroughly enjoying himself.

That first impression has characterized Erk during the many years I have had the privilege of knowing him. He was generally always happy with a great sense of humor. He loved to tell and listen to a good joke.

We coached at Auburn together. We were going out to San Francisco for the national coaching convention and flew together from Columbus to Atlanta. While we were waiting on the airplane in Atlanta, he received a call from Vanderbilt. He left to join Jack Green's staff as the defensive coordinator. I knew he was serious about leaving because he passed up an opportunity to stop by Las Vegas, which we had planned to do.

Erk loved to gamble. Perhaps it was part of his competitive instinct. He loved the horses, the dogs, the cards, and perhaps most of all, rolling the bones. He was always a sight to see at a craps table. His adrenaline was flowing, and he was fun to watch and listen to as he talked to the dice.

When I accepted the head-coaching job here at Georgia, he called me from Atlanta while he was recruiting for Vanderbilt.

"Hey, Vince, how about a job?"

"Hey, Erk, let's talk about it."

It ended up being one of the very best decisions I ever made in my life because he was such a tremendous asset to me, especially during the early days.

I was a young coach who was a hard driver. Erk was a great complement to me because he was older, had more experience, and related much better to the players at Georgia. I was more of a Marine disciplinarian during those early years, which Georgia definitely needed. It was well complemented by Erk and his understanding and compassion.

Erk started out as the defensive coordinator and the defensive ends coach, but after our first game, I felt he would be of more value to us by getting down in the trenches on all fours and coaching the defensive line.

BOTTOM FEEDER

Erk was always the master of the underdog, and I myself enjoyed being in the underdog position. People accused me of always overstating the opponents and understating our ability. I suppose in the final analysis that was true. But it was done in all sincerity because I felt like if you prepared for the worst, then the rest would take care of itself. I wanted to make sure that our team was constantly challenged.

Erk used to always complain that he didn't get the best athletes, which was, of course, an exaggeration. Bill Stanfill, Jake Scott, Jimmy Payne, Freddie Gilbert, Steve Greer, Billy Payne, Eddie "Meat Cleaver" Weaver, Scott Woerner. But, on the other hand, if I did shortchange Erk, which I may have done from time to time, to reinforce our offensive line for example, he would certainly use that more as a motivation factor than anything else with his players.

He always liked for the offense to have the first-class meeting room. He would take the second-class meeting room or any other example that would put his defense in an underdog position.

Erk was a physical fitness enthusiast and felt it was important in light of the fact that he enjoyed his brew. He was always doing pushups, before or after practice. He ran laps, played handball and tennis. He was good at all the sports, though he hated golf while he was at Georgia. We always had a tournament in the spring with the media from the state, and I required the coaches to play a round. Erk didn't even own golf clubs, and he played out of someone else's bag. Now he is an avid golfer and enjoys the game immensely.

He was a particularly good tennis player. I started playing, too, but I took the game up later in life. I improved enough to play with him, but he always beat me. As I challenged Erk, he challenged Dan Magill, our tennis coach and sports information director for many years.

I remember one day Erk played Dan, and Dan whipped him good. I happened by, and Erk was pretty depressed, so he asked me if I would like to play. I played him, and I have never seen him more competitive. He whipped me into the ground and left feeling as good as Dan had earlier. So I was left feeling depressed.

All of a sudden, our trainer, Warren Morris, comes up, and I played him. I was fired up, and I whipped him into the ground. I left happy, and Warren was depressed. I don't know if he ever found anyone to beat that day or not.

Many people remember Erk in pregame warmups actually butting heads with his players. He would scratch that bald head and start to bleed. His blood would really flow, particularly on a hot Saturday afternoon when his adrenaline was flowing. The players would always love to see a coach bleed. It was a tremendous morale boost that got them ready to play.

One of the most embarrassing times of Erk's career was in 1974. Our defensive team was absolutely the worst we have ever had. We had gotten away from some of the basics. We all admit that we didn't do a very good job at coaching. It was a situation that once you got into it, every decision only seemed to make things worse. We ended up at the bottom of the league in every imaginable category of defense. Total defense, scoring defense, rushing defense, pass defense—it didn't make any difference. We were at the bottom.

One writer, David Davidson of *The Atlanta Journal-Constitution*, wrote that Georgia would need a three-digit scoreboard the next year. Erk cut that out and posted it on his desk so he would have to look at it all winter and all spring and all summer in preparation for the 1975 season.

There is no question this was a great motivating factor in the great defenses we had in 1975 and 1976. That was the start of the famous Junkyard Dogs defense.

THE SAME MINDSET

Erk and I basically had the same philosophy about football. If you played good defense and you could run the football and minimize your mistakes and have a sound kicking game and played hard for 60 minutes, then you would be tough to beat. In fact, if you were able to do that, you had a chance in every game no matter how much you might be physically mismatched.

Because we both believed the same philosophy and because we had such mutual respect for each other during the course of the 17 years that we worked together, we had few disagreements and were able to maintain a good working relationship.

Erk was extremely popular with the Georgia people. I allowed him to have his own radio show. I had other head coaches come and tell me that this would be a difficult situation to allow him so many prerogatives and gain that much popularity. Fortunately, I did not take their advice, because I felt comfortable with Erk. I respected him, and I knew that if I were loyal to him, he would in turn be loyal to me.

COACHES AND GODS

In my position of head coach, it was naturally difficult for the players and me to develop a close relationship, but it was important that I gained their respect.

"They didn't like him," John Kasay explained, "because he held them to a high standard. It was not until after they left and saw how unfair the world is, they learned, 'This guy taught us something.'"

But there was something about Erk Russell that players embraced immediately.

"There are coaches, and there are gods," defensive back Bob Kelly opined. "Erk was just unbelievable. I get choked up even thinking about him. He was way beyond a coach."

It was a misconception that Erk berated his players into submission.

"When I talk about him, a lot of people think I'm going to say he was mean," rover Chris Welton said. "You never played for him because you were scared of him. He didn't raise his voice. He was like a good parent. You played for him because you didn't want to disappoint him, not because you were scared of him. The worst thing as a player was to feel that Coach Russell was disappointed in you."

"He could look at you and make you feel like you were Superman," cornerback Mike Fisher said. "You felt elevated when you were around him."

"Erk was classic," Greg Bell recalled. "He kicked us in the ass. He hugged our neck. He had the funniest jokes. He kept us motivated. Erk took a bunch of guys who were kind of plain and turned them into the Junkyard Dogs."

Defensive lineman Tim Crowe's experience of playing under Erk is such that he puts his father and Erk in the same category.

"Anything he said, you thought you could do," Crowe said. "He always had a story to tell. When you sit and watch films, there was never a dull moment. He and [newspaper humorist and Georgia alumnus] Lewis Grizzard had the same brain. He would be a great dad. In fact, to this day if I see him, it is just like seeing my dad."

THE PROOF

Erk Russell could inspire confidence in his players to the point that they did impossible things, and Tim Crowe has the story to prove it.

One of the more tedious requirements of practice was to hit a sled up against a wall. The players despised the drill. It was boring, and the sled was heavy.

One day in practice, Erk told tackle Jimmy Payne, "Jimmy, if you break this thing, we won't hit it the rest of the year."

Payne slammed into the sled with such ferocity that he did indeed break it.

"Coach Russell was a man of his word," Crowe said. "We didn't have to hit it all year."

THE CREATIVE LEADER

Linebacker Frank Ros, who became an executive with Coca-Cola, studied Erk Russell in developing his own leadership habits.

"He was the master of creating rallying points," Ros said. "He did it at Georgia Southern."

Erk left Georgia after the 1981 spring practice to start a new program at Georgia Southern. His creativity brought tradition to a program that had none. For example, a creek—actually it was little more than a drainage ditch—ran near the practice field in Statesboro. Erk dubbed it Eagle Creek. Whenever the Eagles went on the road, they took a jar of Eagle Creek water to mark their territory on the visitors' fields.

THE G.A.

Rusty Russell, Erk's son, was our graduate assistant that year, working with Wayne McDuffie and John Kasay on the offensive line. All graduate assistants add something valuable, but he was unique in that he came from such a great coaching background. That gave us an extra benefit.

He walked on, just like his brother Jay did. I admire both of them. Rusty came here from Florida State. He had gone down there for a year and was not happy. He wanted to be around Georgia football. He came back and played in the early 1970s and earned a scholarship. So did Jay.

Jay was a wide receiver, but he was hurt in 1980 and missed the season, but we gave him a letter anyway. He was part of the team.

THE VOLUNTEER

The rules allowed each school one volunteer coach. He could not recruit, but otherwise he could participate as a coach in any other way. Because of the emphasis we put on the kicking game, Bill Hartman, our volunteer coach, coached our kickers and punters.

Coach Hartman had played as a back at Georgia in the late 1930s and then played one year in the NFL. He later came back and coached until 1956 under Wally Butts before he started a successful insurance career. As the backfield coach under Coach Butts, he coached the famed Georgia duo of Frank Sinkwich and Charley Trippi.

From the day I arrived at Georgia, he became a friend and has been a friend over 40-plus years. I got him out to coach the kickers after the third or fourth year I was here. He was the perfect fit. Kickers are usually out there by themselves until you call them, and they need supervision. He gave them that.

Coach Hartman worked with the specialists on a daily basis, and while we worked on some aspect of the kicking game every day in practice, most of the practice they were on their own.

He had a regular format he followed. He had been a punter in college, so he understood the principles of kicking, and he always compared it to golf.

"The swing is not brute power," he said. "It is getting your foot on the ball properly."

The kickers would start on the two-yard line hash mark and kick 10 out of 10 through the uprights. If there were five kickers, all five of them would kick. Then they went to the right hash at the nine-yard line and kicked five for five. Then they went to the left hash to the 18-yard line to kick five out of five.

They would end up with a contest to see who could win the game with a 50-yard field goal.

But even with the number of kickers we had on the team, this was not enough to eat up the whole practice. So to keep the players interested, Coach Hartman taught them to run the Notre Dame Box. That was the offense he had played.

"That did two things," Coach Hartman explained. "It gave them a lot of exercise for 15 minutes that they would not have gotten otherwise. They were not just standing around. And it kept them interested.

"They all learned the Notre Dame Box. We would take the various kickers and alternate them at end, tailback, quarterback, fullback, right half, left half. The great play in the Notre Dame Box is Shift Left 65-2, which is a spinner, half spinner to the fullback going back to the right, crossing the ends and sending the left halfback up the gut."

Coach Hartman also put in trick plays. When Kevin Butler was our kicker, they had a play where the holder, Jim Broadway, would get up with the snap and run an option pitch to Butler, who would throw to the right end. He wanted me to use that in a game, but I never did.

Coach Hartman was an advocate for the kickers. Kickers are such a strange breed. They go out there when the game is on the line, and they become a hero or a goat.

Of the coaches who coach contact football, very few of them understand kickers. As soon as one would mess up, at the next staff meeting you would get all these expert opinions about kickers. "Change kickers." "Get so-and-so in here." "He can't kick." Nobody defends them, but Coach Hartman did.

He was the one who would always stand up for them when all these expert contact coaches are talking about the kickers. He was a very valuable resource in that respect.

Once they threw out the volunteer coach because people abused it, he went back to school and became a graduate assistant for three years in order to coach for three more years. He was in his 80s then.

Chapter Three

RECRUITING

PUTTING THE PUZZLE TOGETHER

When Alabama beat Auburn to win the Southeastern Conference championship in 1979, it meant that Georgia would not be going bowling.

Recruiting became our top priority.

And that meant that backfield coach Mike Cavan moved to Wrightsville, Georgia—literally.

Mike moved into a cabin owned by Wrightsville car dealer Bob Newsome. He moved to Wrightsville for one reason: to sign Herschel Walker.

"We all felt we needed a running back," Mike said, "and the other thing—the big thing at the time—was that we had lost William Andrews, James Brooks, George Rogers.... Everyone from Georgia had gone out of state."

We could not keep letting these players leave the state. Nobody knew for sure what kind of player Walker would be, but the perception was that we could not let another one get away.

THE FIRST MEETING

Now, when I think about the first time I met Herschel Walker, what comes to mind right away is his being over on the sidelines, seeing him for the first time and introducing him to Willie McClendon. I remember McClendon looking at him and being impressed with Walker's physical stature.

Of course, McClendon had by then become a real tailback. In 1978 he broke the Georgia single-season rushing record that Frank Sinkwich had set back in 1941. And Walker was the guy who was going to replace McClendon and break his record in one year.

It was interesting to see the humility of Walker as he paid McClendon great respect. At the same time, I was also impressed with McClendon looking at Walker and recognizing that this was a special athlete.

Of course, I went to see Walker on several occasions while he was in high school. You hear so much that you don't get too over-ly excited when someone says, "We have got a great player." I have heard it a thousand times. But we kept hearing it again and again. So when we went to see him firsthand, we could see that this was not just a normal "we have got a good one here."

BUT COULD HE PLAY WITH THE BIG BOYS?

What set Herschel Walker apart was his rare combination of size and speed. He was six foot one and 222 pounds and had twice won the 100-yard dash high school state championship in Class A.

Mike Cavan thought he was a great high school back, but he never claimed that Walker would be an immediate solution or that he would be even an All-America running back.

"All I ever said was he was the biggest, fastest person I had ever seen play," Mike recalled. "Everybody kept saying he was only play-ing Class A ball. Well, he didn't move there. He was born there. It wasn't like he was trying to play there. Don't hold that against him.

"Again, he was the biggest, fastest guy I ever saw. It was amazing. He was as big as a senior in high school—he was always 222 pounds—as he was in college. He never varied. He was a man among boys there.

"To say that any of us thought he would be a Heisman winner… you wanted that to happen. You wanted to think he could take you over the hump."

WALKER DRAWS A CROWD

Herschel Walker was the most famous high school football player in the state of Georgia in 1979. His high school statistics were huge, and his measurable abilities were well documented. And everybody wanted him.

"His junior year I saw him play a couple of times," Mike Cavan recalled. "I spent some time down there when he was a junior. When he was a senior, I saw 14 of his 15 games. The one game I did not see was when Johnson County got beat."

Herschel Walker was a world-class sprinter who was at the top of many schools' recruiting lists. *Photo by Tim Gentry*

Mike had other players to recruit as well, and one of them was Tommy Thurson, a linebacker in Jacksonville, Florida. Mike had promised Thurson that he would go see him play.

"That was the night Johnson County got beat by Emanuel County Institute in little Twin City, Georgia," he recalled. "They got beat 3-0. Somebody should have gone down there and found out how they did it."

Later in the playoffs Johnson County beat ECI by close to 50 points.

Graduate assistant coach Rusty Russell saw Walker in the game they lost. When he got back, he told Mike, "He didn't look very good."

Mike said Rusty was not going back to Wrightsville.

THE RECRUITING DIRECTOR GETS INVOLVED

Steve Greer, as our recruiting director, was also involved in the day-to-day recruiting of Herschel Walker.

"It was a long, drawn-out deal," Steve recalled. "I had recruited Herschel a little bit when I was at Auburn. When I came to Georgia in 1979, Mike [Cavan] had that territory."

All that really meant was that Steve did not move to Wrightsville quite as quickly as Mike. He waited until January 2. Mike was already down there during the Christmas holidays.

The two would alternate coming back to Athens to see their families. But they spent a lot of time in Wrightsville. But even in Athens they could not escape Walker.

"There were many, many times I can remember at 2 a.m. the phone would ring. 'Steve, this is Vince, call me back in five minutes.'

"I'm trying to wake up, and my wife would ask, 'Who the hell was that? You are *not* going to Wrightsville again! Nobody is worth this much trouble!'"

I would say, "Steve, I think you need to drive on back to Wrightsville and be ready to talk to that boy at 8 a.m."

I was always thinking of new things to say to him.

So Steve would drive to Wrightsville and wake up Mike with, "Here is what we have to say today."

Mike Cavan was the coach in charge of recruiting Herschel Walker for Georgia.

EGG ON THE MEDIA

Because there was no motel in Wrightsville, Mike Cavan and Steve Greer had an advantage with their housing at the Bob Newsome cabin. Rival coaches stayed at a motel some 18 miles up the road, or perhaps in Macon, which led to a big mistake in the Atlanta newspaper.

The recruiting battle for Herschel Walker was one of the hot stories in the papers. There were always rumors.

One of the great stories is the Southern Cal rumor about Trojans coach John Robinson.

The Atlanta paper had gotten a tip that Southern Cal was going to sign Walker. There were always rumors, but the reporters felt it was reliable. They got a tip that Robinson had checked into the Hilton Hotel in Macon. So they called the hotel and found out that John Robinson was checked in, so they said, "Run it!"

It was in the headlines of the paper. It might have been on the front page. "Herschel to sign with Southern Cal."

But it happened to be that this John Robinson was some sales-man from South Georgia. That was the biggest egg in the face of any speculation by the news media.

THE WALKER WATCH

Steve Greer and Mike Cavan had a daily routine in Wrightsville. "The mailman had a couple of old bird dogs," Steve said. "We would go bird hunting in the morning. Then we would go to the school and have lunch with Herschel, watch basketball practice or the game if he was playing that night. Then the next day the same routine."

They were not the only coaches doing that.

"Clemson was there quite a bit," Mike said. "Chuck Reedy, who ended up being a head coach at Baylor, was there as much as I was."

"We'd have volleyball games with all of the assistant coaches," Steve said. "What else are you going to do in Wrightsville? You look around, and there sat UCLA, Southern Cal, South Carolina, Clemson, Auburn."

THE FINAL THREE

Herschel Walker was being pursued not only by college coach-es, but by reporters, each of whom wanted to be the one to break the story. Eventually, one of them reported that Walker had nar-rowed his schools down to three, but he did not say which three.

"It was late in the process when he had come out in the paper that he had narrowed his choices to three teams," Mike Cavan said. "Steve [Greer] didn't have any patience at all."

With six to eight colleges still hanging around every day, Steve grew impatient. He hatched a plan to have Walker announce to the audience of coaches who his final three schools were. Mike was against the idea.

"Steve, don't put that guy on the spot," Mike pleaded. "Suppose he tells us to go home? I'm not going home."

But Steve followed through with his plan.

"I'll never forget," Mike winced. "There was Clemson, Southern Cal, UCLA, Georgia Tech. It was a damn coaching convention."

"Herschel," Steve said, "we have all these guys around here. You have said you have narrowed your choices to three schools. We are all grown men. You need to cut everybody else loose."

Walker's response caught everybody off guard. In fact, somewhere in his reply was a reference to Fidel Castro and Cuba, which didn't seem pertinent to the question.

That was enough for Mike, who looked at Steve, "You stupid— get out of here. Everything is fine. Herschel, I'll see you tomorrow." Mike wanted to kill Steve.

THE BEGINNINGS OF A TRACK AND FIELD PROGRAM

Aside from in-state connections, Georgia had one other edge on other schools in recruiting Herschel Walker. His sister, Veronica, was on a track and field scholarship at Georgia.

But that, too, is an interesting story.

Veronica was a year older than Walker. Mike saw her training with the girls' track and field team.

"She was as impressive as a girl athlete as Herschel was as a guy," he said.

Mike's heart jumped up in his throat when Gary Phillips, the high school coach at Johnson County, reported that Clemson and Tennessee had offered track scholarships to Veronica. Mike rushed to Phillips's office to call me with that news.

I asked him, "Mike, do you suppose that if we sign her, we will get Herschel?"

"It's not 100 percent, but it couldn't hurt us," Mike replied.

Mike was confused because we didn't have a girls' track team, so he mentioned that to me.

"We'll just start a women's track program," I said.

Veronica was a legitimate track athlete. It's true we did not have a women's track program, but we were going to add one in our plan. I would have to say we moved the plan up a year. We had an outstanding athlete with whom we could kick off the program.

"That was a very big decision made quickly," Mike reflected. "I think it was more to do with Title IX. They were pressuring us to do something, and this gave us a reason to do it, and we did it. She came in and was a tremendous athlete in her own right, and I think she was an All-American and married one of our All-America track guys."

THE DECISIVE COIN TOSS

To this day, Herschel Walker maintains that he came to Georgia because of a coin toss.

"To be honest, those stories are true," he said. "I flipped a coin. As a kid you are naïve and stupid. You don't realize what you are doing. A lot of people were saying, 'Herschel, we want you at Georgia.' I'm thinking I need to be somewhere else. They were saying, 'No, you need to come to Georgia.'

"So I decided, if they are going to tell me where to go, I'm going to flip a coin. So I really did end up flipping a coin. It was best out of five, because I had two other teams, and Georgia was winning. Then I pulled the names out of bag, and it came up Georgia.

"What is funny, I told my parents that day, and they got so excited they called the Georgia coaches 'He has decided to come to Georgia.' But I hadn't decided. I just said that to get them off my case. I ended up signing that night, not really sure what I was going to do. I was too embarrassed to say, 'Hey, guys, that was a joke.'"

SPOILED HOLIDAY

Herschel Walker was the last major player in the country to sign that year. He signed on Easter Sunday.

Barbara and I—really Barbara—had planned a family trip to go to Boston. Barbara's brother was in Boston, and she had been talking about this trip for a long time, and I said, "Yes, yes, yes, go ahead and plan the trip." And then it got to be about Thursday, and I said, "Barbara, I can't go." You can imagine the reaction.

"What do you mean you can't go?"

"Herschel hasn't signed yet."

"To heck with Herschel!" she said. "Who does he think he is? We have planned this trip for three months, and now I have to go up there with four children on my own?"

It almost broke up a marriage again.

But she went on up to Boston, and I was here.

Well, it was Easter morning. I was in the office, and Steve Greer came up. He was as nervous as a cat. He couldn't even speak. He couldn't get a word out of his mouth.

"What is it?" I asked.

"Herschel is ready to sign."

"Let's go."

So we left for Wrightsville. Because of the fact that we had used all of our visits, we couldn't go into the house until after he had signed. We had to stay outside.

"I ended up signing to come to Georgia," Walker remembered. "Believing in the Lord Jesus, the Lord will lay out a path for you. All you have to do is follow it. There is no doubt that coming here was the best thing for me. If you let the Lord handle it, He will put you in the right place."

CHANGED OPINIONS

Fast-forward to the night after the Tennessee game, when Herschel Walker had come off the bench to score two touch-downs and help rally Georgia to a 16-15 win.

The coaches' wives rode in a van to Tennessee. These were the same wives who had been exasperated by the seemingly never-ending recruitment of Herschel.

The first thing they said when they got back to Athens and saw their husbands was, "That son of a gun *is* worth it!"

THE CAPTAIN

Frank Ros was the captain of the 1980 team. Not only was he the captain, he was probably one of the best we ever had. And he is the captain today. He is the one who has formed the reunion. He is the one who gets them back together. He is the one who is there when there are problems to deal with.

He was a senior that year. He was one of those persistent play-ers who became by far the best conditioned athlete we ever had. Nobody competed with him for the best conditioned athlete. They competed for the second best conditioned athlete, because they almost automatically gave him that position. They knew he was going to be the best conditioned athlete. It was a fact. Point-wise, the way we did it, which was a combination of things, endurance and weights that all added up to points, he was just not going to be beat. That was how he gained his respect. It was an extremely important part of the team.

Ros grew up a fan of the Gamecocks.

"I would have gone to South Carolina blindly," he said. "I would have gone out of ignorance. It was just divine intervention that Georgia even recruited me."

PALMETTO PIPELINE

Frank Ros was not the only key player on the 1980 team who came from South Carolina. We had Jeff Hipp, our safety; Pat McShea, a defensive end; and Carnie "Poochie" Norris, a backup tailback.

Hipp grew up in West Columbia, South Carolina, but he was a Clemson fan. We got him because Clemson was a little down that year.

McShea was from Anderson, South Carolina. He played at T.L. Hanna High, the school featured in the movie *Radio*. Frank Inman stumbled across him because Hanna had a good quarterback at the time. We didn't get the quarterback, but we got McShea.

SOUTH OF THE BORDER

We always had good fortune recruiting out of the state of Florida, and that year was no exception. That team had Eddie Weaver from Haines City, Tim Morrison from Live Oak, Joe Creamons from Eustis, and Tommy Thurson from Jacksonville.

Morrison saw an opportunity to play right away as an offensive lineman.

"Georgia was graduating some senior players, and I didn't want to ride the pine," he said.

We struggled to a 5-6 record his first year in 1977, and Morrison told me it was his fault because he had played on a losing program in high school.

Mike Cavan recruited Thurson the same year that he signed Walker.

"Mike was like a brother to me," Thurson said, whose real brother, Ted, was at Georgia Tech. "Mike was one of the biggest reasons I came to Georgia."

Thurson also liked the fact that Georgia didn't just try to show him a good time when he came for his visit. We showed him that we were interested in him as a student as well.

Creamons grew up a fan of the Florida Gators. His father went to school there, and Creamons went to a lot of the Georgia–Florida games in the 1970s, always pulling for Florida. But we won him over with a chance to play for Erk Russell.

He visited us when we shut out Alabama in 1976, still one of the loudest days ever at Sanford Stadium. Creamons had played the night before and had something like 18 tackles and four sacks, and Erk offered him a scholarship the morning of the game.

"I wanted to think about it," Creamons recalled. "But I was so impressed with the facilities and the players and the coaches that I committed Sunday morning. I canceled a trip to Ohio State."

His decision was not well received in Eustis, a Gator hotbed.

"I went from being the greatest defensive tackle in Eustis history to the worst in one day," Creamons said. "People would call the house and leave nasty messages."

THE HOMETOWN CONNECTION

Georgia has had a lot of hometown boys make good as Bulldogs. Fran Tarkenton, Andy Johnson, Jeff Pyburn, and Paul Gilbert were starting quarterbacks. So was David Dukes for a while, though he found his niche as a punter. We had a couple of local boys who kicked for us, Steve Crumley and John Kasay.

The 1980 team had two local boys, Anthony Arnold at flanker and Jimmy Payne at defensive tackle.

We almost lost Payne to Tennessee. Erk Russell was recruiting him.

"He came as close to getting me fired as anybody ever has," Erk joked.

"He was my prospect at Cedar Shoals, and he committed to Tennessee. We couldn't allow that to happen. I had gone to see him play basketball, I don't know how many times. Everywhere they went, I was there, and I thought we really had the guy."

But Tennessee made a run at Payne late in the recruiting process and swayed him. Erk countered.

"Jimmy, you can't go to Tennessee," Erk said. "You are a natural resource of this community, and you've got to stay here."

That must have worked, because he signed with Georgia.

"But I really believe I would have been fired if he had gone to Tennessee," Erk confessed. "And his daddy, James, worked for the athletic department!"

Well, I would not have fired Erk, but I would have been very unhappy. After all, Payne's dad was on the grounds crew. James helped me in the athletic director's box on game day until he retired.

Besides, I was the one who bought Payne his first pair of football shoes when he was 12 years old, long before I ever knew he was going to be a college prospect.

James cames to me one day at practice to borrow $20 to buy Payne his first pair of cleats. James paid me back a year later. I am sure our competitors would have charged me with illegal recruiting had they known the story. But it really wasn't, plus the statute of limitations had run out!

Payne became an All-American and played professional football briefly before injuries short-circuited his career. He died of cancer in November 1998.

"Jimmy Payne was a great American," Erk said. "It is too bad he had the tough luck that he had. He was just a great guy to coach, and he would do anything I asked him to do."

THE TRANSFERS

Transfers were never a big part of our recruiting, but that team did have a few, including a couple who walked on and earned scholarships.

Three players in our defensive backfield transferred in: Bob Kelly, Dale Williams, and Mike Fisher. Williams came from The Citadel, and the other two from Furman.

Fisher had a scholarship at Furman. He had played high school ball in Jacksonville, Florida, with one of our players, Gordon Terry, but we did not recruit him. But he would come up some and watch Terry play. The desire to play big-time college football was born on those visits.

"We washed our own shirts at Furman," he said, "and the facilities were not nearly what they are at Georgia. Furman just seemed a bit of a letdown."

After he came to Georgia, he played through the 1978 season as a walk-on. He got a loan from an aunt in Chattanooga to pay his tuition one quarter.

He had a good spring in 1979. I called him to my office. He was trying to think of what he had done wrong, but I told him he had earned a scholarship.

"It was one of the highlights of my memory," Fisher said.

One of the lowlights came later that summer when Chip Wisdom had to call him and tell him that we were taking the scholarship away.

"Chip said something about they had given away too many," Fisher recalled. "I was demolished. Floored. I cried for hours. I couldn't believe it. I knew I was going to play. I regrouped and went back and emphasized that I would be back."

When I gave him a scholarship originally, I told him, "Mike, I want you to understand that the scholarship is available this year, but it may not be available next year, and if we are over, I may have to take it away."

Herschel Walker (34) and Jimmy Payne (87) were named to the *Playboy* **All-America team together.**

And it just so happened that we were over. So I remember calling him. There were about three or four who were in the same boat. I reminded him of what I had told him. I'll never forget his response.

"Coach, that will be the biggest mistake you've ever made in your whole life."

As it turned out, we were able to keep him on scholarship. Of course, it ended up he made some big plays for us in 1980.

Kelly loved Georgia and wanted to come, but we made no offer to him. So he went to Furman. He played some on special teams and in the secondary. When his coach took a position at North Carolina State, he offered to take Kelly along.

Figuring he might transfer anyway, Kelly decided to explore his opportunities. He went to Florida State and shared a brief conversation with Bobby Bowden, and he came to Athens, where he met with Erk Russell and Sam Mitchell, the secondary coach then.

"They were not going to give me a scholarship, but they gave me some encouragement," Kelly said. "Georgia was loaded with seniors that year so I wasn't going to play anyway."

As it developed, many of those seniors were injured during spring practice, and Kelly played a lot with the first-team defense. So early that summer I called his home.

"Bob, I have a question for you. Would you be interested in going on scholarship next year?"

It was a rhetorical question, of course.

We also had a transfer in the offensive line in Joe Happe. He was from Jenkintown, Pennsylvania, an area we would not normally recruit. He went to Wake Forest as a freshman, but he transferred after one year there to go to a junior college. Happe said that one of the big reasons he came to Georgia was because of how impressed he was with Hugh Nall, another lineman. What makes that interesting is that Nall and Happe were going to compete for playing time at the same position.

"Hugh went out of his way to recruit me," Happe said, "which blew my mind."

BEATING OUT SAM HOUSTON STATE

The recruiting of Herschel Walker indirectly led to a signing that was all but overlooked when it took place. But Terry Hoage eventually became one of our greatest defensive football players ever.

Hoage was not on our recruiting list. A professor at Sam Houston State in Huntsville, Texas, kept pestering us that we needed to recruit him. His name was Dr. Richard Payne. He kept calling Steve Greer. He must have called half a dozen times.

Dr. Payne was a Georgia guy, and he was a friend of Hoage's father. Hoage was the kind of player that I was looking for. I wanted to find someone who was overlooked, was a good student and of good character, and could be around our program throughout his college career and maybe contribute his third and fourth year.

Stricken with cabin fever in Wrightsville, Steve and Mike Cavan agreed that a scouting expedition to Huntsville was just what they needed.

"Anything to get out of there," Steve said.

The drive to Atlanta, the flight to Houston, and the drive to Huntsville might otherwise have been laborious. But for those two, it was like a vacation.

They were warmly received by the Huntsville coach, who gave a rundown on his prospects, some already committed to other schools.

"What about Terry Hoage?" Steve asked.

"I think he's going to Harvard," the coach replied.

They both looked at film and were impressed enough to send new secondary coach Bill Lewis back to Texas the following week.

Hoage was a quarterback his senior year, which been marred by injury. His season was over with by the time Bill arrived in Hunstville, but he saw him play basketball.

"It seemed like every loose ball he got," Lewis remembered. "I met his family and was very impressed with how bright he was.

"I watched his tape, and I could tell he was a pretty good high school quarterback. It wasn't enough to say I saw a great player, but I saw a special individual.

"He had a lot of intangible qualities that you fell in love with," Lewis said. "Terry just fit. He was a bright guy, tough and eager."

Hoage eventually became a two-time All-America defensive back. I always said that particular class had the nation's most sought-after player in Herschel Walker and the least sought-after in Terry Hoage. Both of them became consensus All-Americans.

But his contribution in 1980 boiled down to a single play. But what a play it was!

SOUTH GEORGIA CONNECTION

Valdosta High School has an unbelievable high school tradition in football. And a lot of very good college football players have come out of that program. Buck Belue, our quarterback, was one of them.

Belue was highly sought after in high school. He was a fine baseball player, too, but football was his first love. As it developed, there was a wide receiver from nearby Jesup, Georgia, Lindsay Scott, and we recruited them together. Everybody did.

They did not know each other that well in high school, but they were thrown together as recruits, often visiting schools together.

Belue committed first, after leading Valdosta to the state finals in 1977, where they lost in Athens to Clarke Central. Belue's commitment in turn influenced Scott.

"As a receiver, I wanted to go somewhere where I was going to be more involved and showcase my ability," Scott said. "Buck had a special talent, and he was the kind of person I wanted to play with. When he signed with Georgia, it raised my eyebrows. I knew what he could do."

I met Scott outside John Donaldson's house in Jesup. John was on my first staff at Georgia, but he was Scott's high school coach by then. He was just a sophomore then. I was just relaxing at John's house when Scott came by, so we were able to meet before the recruiting process took shape.

Scott had an immediate impact as a freshman. He ran a kickoff back 99 yards at LSU to help us win in Baton Rouge in 1978, and he was a starter most of his freshman and sophomore years.

It was more difficult for Belue. He didn't play much as a freshman in 1978. We had a veteran, Jeff Pyburn, at quarterback, and the team was playing well.

"It was tough on him," Scott recalled. "A lot of freshmen go through that. They had a veteran quarterback, and when push comes to shove, they were going to go with the older guy, the more seasoned guy."

"He was going to leave Georgia," said Greg Bell, one year older than Belue. "He was talking to me about how frustrated he was. I was the big sophomore talking to him about hanging in there. A few weeks later he leads us on a big comeback against Georgia Tech."

Belue still recalls that 29-28 comeback win over Georgia Tech as one of his biggest wins, probably because it was the first significant minutes he played as the Georgia quarterback. He led us to one of the most amazing comebacks in Georgia football history, climaxed by a sensational fourth-down touchdown pass to Anthony Arnold, followed up by a two-point option pitch to Arnold to win the game. But Georgia fans will point to another play as their favorite Buck Belue moment.

Chapter Four

PRACTICE

ERK'S PRESEASON CALENDAR

While others on the team stayed in Athens that summer to work out along with the five caught stealing the pig, it was not as common then for all players to stay on campus all year long.

Defensive coordinator Erk Russell always sent out a schedule to the players, reminding them to exercise and train properly for the upcoming season. His calendar for 1980 read as follows:

Friday, August 1: 3,000 years ago, Moses said: "Take up your tent and get off your ass. We're going to the Promised Land." Today, I say to you, "Take up your running shoes and get off your ass. We're going to the Sugar Bowl."

Saturday, August 2: Today's poem: There is a young coach named Kase/Who wears a big smile on his face/My test is great/I can hardly wait/For you and the big two-mile race.

Sunday, August 3: Go to church: Select a church two miles away. Run there in thirteen minutes. After church, run home in twelve minutes.

Monday, August 4: "Straight arrow" Nall says: Join Hudson, Woerner, Ros, Welton & me in going Hog Wild about beating everybody in 1980. We're in the best condition ever. How about you?

Tuesday, August 5: Your horoscope: The alignment of the stars indicates that you will make several short trips soon. May I suggest about twenty 40-yard sprints today! Eighth in SEC?

Wednesday, August 6: Humor for today: Morrison: Do you know what has 16 balls and sings? Harper: No. Morrison: A male quartet. Harper: That's only eight balls, stupid. Morrison: One of them is a Tenor. Have you run tenor twelve miles this week?

Thursday, August 7: *Don't be a glutton: A glutton is one who eats fried chicken all day and wakes up in the middle of the night with a breast in one hand and a thigh in the other. How is your weight?*

Friday, August 8: *If it is to be, it is up to me. The best day—Today. The best time—Now. The best person to do the job—ME.*

Saturday, August 9: *The epitome of living. There ain't nothing like being a Bulldog on a Saturday night after winning a football game.*

Sunday, August 10: *Go to church: Do not hate Tenn. while in Church (23 hours will be adequate today). A hard workout this afternoon will be good for the soul, brother.*

Monday, August 11: *A fact of life: Work a little—win a little. Work a lot—win a lot. No deposit—no return. Run! Run! Run!*

Tuesday, August 12: *First sunrise service will be held one week from today for those who feel the feel. Will You Be There?*

Wednesday, August 13: *Get a big neck: Do neck Iso with Earnest. If Earnest is not available, do neck bridges with Gusto. A player's best friend is a big neck!*

Thursday, August 14: *Rope a dope: Womack: Did you hear the story about the rope? Stewart: No, Jimmy. Womack: Skip it! Then run like crazy.*

Friday, August 15: *Welcome Home! Your kind, friendly, thoughtful, courteous coaches are anxiously awaiting your arrival. Please drive carefully! Three days till the test!*

Saturday, August 16: *Pictures and physicals. The cameras are ready. Dr. Hubert is ready. Is your body ready?*

LAST CHANCE FOR THE SENIORS

Your four years as a college football player can go by awfully fast, and the days never seem as short as during your last year. Forced to stay in Athens for the summer because of his part in the swine escapade, senior rover Chris Welton tried to make the best of it.

"Back then most people went home during the summer, except guys who needed to be in summer school to be eligible," he said. "Our class had an up-and-down career. We got there and were part of Coach Dooley's only losing season. Then we had a good run, but a disappointing finish our sophomore year, tying Auburn and losing in the Bluebonnet Bowl. In our junior year I got hurt and missed the last seven games. I tore up my knee. We ended up being 6-5 and losing to everybody in the ACC.

"I think all of us would say we sure liked the good year better than the two bad years. Plus we had never beaten Auburn. We had lost one to Georgia Tech and beat them twice, and we had things to do. Other than Scott Woerner, none of us in the secondary thought we had another year in football. Giving up a few months didn't seem like such a big deal."

THE HARD WORK BEGINS

I will never forget the arrival of Herschel Walker that summer. As I arrived at the Coliseum to go to my office at 6:15 a.m., I saw this black car drive by. It was Walker! He evidently got up at 2 a.m. and couldn't sleep and left Wrightsville at 4 a.m. It seemed strange to see him driving around the Coliseum several hours before he was due to report.

It was traditional that the freshmen carry the bags of the upper-classmen. So he was there early. He would grab bags and run them up the steps. He got some points, but they had heard so much about him, they were anxious to find out how good this freshman was going to be.

The first impression Walker made was that he was a respectful person.

"He understood the process that all freshmen had to go through," guard Tim Morrison remembered.

"He was down to earth," defensive end Robert Miles said. "He wasn't country, but you knew he was from a rural area. You could talk about going on a trip, but you could tell that he had not been there and done that too many times.

"But we had a lot of guys from small towns, so it was no big deal. In practice, if we had to pick up the cones, he grabbed one just like everybody else."

You are hopeful and optimistic before every season begins, and that season was no different. We felt like we were going to have a good football team. We were solid. We did have that missing piece of the puzzle, which was a tailback, if Walker would fill that void, maybe with time. I thought as the season went on he might really help us, but quite frankly I didn't think he would be a big factor that soon. I never dreamed he would have such an immediate impact.

PUTTING THE CLOCK ON WALKER

Line coach John Kasay was also in charge of conditioning. When the players went through physical tests at the start of practice, he directed the tests.

"When we were timing in the 40, I used to like for all the coaches to be down on the finish line," John said. He didn't want any complaining from fellow staff members that he was bending the times.

Herschel Walker warmed up like the trackman that he was, which meant that he took his time stretching.

"Most of those track guys, it takes a day and a half to warm up," John shouted. "A day and a half! You have to be tired by the time you warm up."

Walker stretched and twisted and stretched and twisted some more. Finally John told him, "Let's run."

As always, he ran with an effortless style, belying his size.

When he reached the finish line, you could hear the watches clicking.

"Click, click, click," John demonstrated. "It should sound simultaneous."

John looked down at my watch, and the number staring back at him was less was 4.3 seconds.

"4.27," he recalled, "But I wasn't going to say anything."

The other coaches looked at their watches, and they were looking at similar numbers. No one was telling what the time was, but it seemed too fast.

"Ah, let him run it again!" someone shouted.

Walker's second run was just as efficient and just as fast.

John's watch registered 4.26 on the second run.

Mike Cavan looked at his watch and said, "That is the fastest guy I have *ever* seen!"

"From that time on, he had our attention," John deadpanned.

WELCOME TO THE SEC!

The veteran players built the freshmen up off the field and knocked them down on the field. The freshmen were usually on the third floor, and the veterans would inflate their egos.

"We heard about you!"

"You made All-State!"

"You've got some huge arms!"

"How fast are you?"

Cornerback Greg Bell said, "We would really blow them up. There are several things a man lies about, and one of them is how fast he is, and another one is how strong he is.

"They were all going to be Heisman Trophy winners."

In the locker room each day, the veterans would pick somebody as their target for the day. Herschel Walker was no exception. He got his "Welcome to the SEC."

Eddie Weaver administered the first hit on Walker, a ferocious head-on collision during a drill. It has grown to legendary proportions since then.

"Herschel got killed by Eddie and Frank Ros and a bunch of other guys, and they loved every minute of it," linebackers coach Chip Wisdom said. "Herschel took his licks and just trotted back to huddle. It didn't faze him really. Anybody who thought that guy was going to be our savior for the season would have had to have had his head examined."

Defensive end Pat McShea remembered it the same way.

"I only remember one inside drill when he ran straight ahead and 'Meat Cleaver' hit him pretty good," McShea said. "I didn't get to see much of him. I know I didn't see much that stood out until he came in that first game."

Of course, Walker was the most heralded of the newcomers, and everyone had heard of him. He attracted a lot of attention in practice.

"We had a lot of guys who had come through who were supposed to be hot stuff," linebacker Frank Ros noted. "By the time you are a junior or senior, all that stuff goes out the window. Plus Herschel was thrown to the wolves against the No. 1 defense in the country that year."

Coming from Pennsylvania via a Virginia junior college, guard Joe Happe was unfamiliar with Walker.

"I knew he was the top recruit, and there was a lot of hype as he reported," Happe said. "But in preseason he had a very average practice early on. We stopped looking at him. Our attitude was, he's going to be good, but he is not going to be phenomenal. He will help us down the road. We decided he was just normal."

John Kasay surmised that Walker was not accustomed to such a high level of practice.

"He just didn't seem to understand how we practiced," John explained, "because he had never practiced before. Down in Wrightsville, what are they going to do, let him get tired? No, they let him get tired on Friday nights, which he did, running 40, 50, and 60 yards a play.

"But he was the best kid. He would be sitting there 30 minutes before every meeting started, fully dressed. How many kids do that today? That was the kind of guy he was. He put everything else out of his mind. He went to school, and he played football. That was all."

"People always ask what it was like to tackle Herschel," rover Chris Welton said. "Well, the only times I ever tackled him were in that period and maybe one or two practices in bowl scrimmage. In that period, he was not impressive. He was tiptoeing around. I was as surprised as anyone when we got up to Knoxville. When you hit him, you felt the power, the strength. You thought physically he was gifted. But in summer camp I never saw him turn it on. In practice he was not impressive. I think he was unsure of what he was doing. He was tentative."

Bell remembers that the prognosis was even darker.

"When he came, he had a problem," Bell said. "He ran upright. In college you learn to use leverage, and they teach you how to tackle differently. Because of his running style, which was straight up, you could nail him.

"We had these special drills with these hand dummies and he would run the line, and we would swat him at the waist to try to get him to bend those shoulders over, and he just wouldn't do it. It was hopeless. The coaches were concerned.

"I remember one scrimmage we had after the first week when I was playing left cornerback, the line opened up and I filled in the gap, and here he came. I put the crosshairs right there and boom, you take him backward, and it was no big whoop.

"We beat on him the first week and a half unmercifully. We tortured him, and to his credit, he never griped and he never complained."

Safety Jeff Hipp, however, once came face to face with Walker and discovered that he was a powerful runner.

"I hit him one time, and he actually caved my facemask in," he laughed. "I had to change the headgear, because he unloaded on me."

Backup safety Bob Kelly had a similar encounter.

"Herschel came up the middle one time, and the impact was like tackling a Volkswagen," he said. "I completely popped my hamstring. I was not even going to travel to the first game except that Coach Lewis took me along as an 'atta boy' for hanging in there."

INTERESTED OBSERVER

As often as possible, UGA president Fred Davison visited practice. He was a friend, a great football fan, and a tremendous supporter of college athletics. He wanted Georgia to compete at the highest level. Yet at the same time, he was very conscious about raising the academic standards.

He and I were involved in a summit meeting on Sapelo Island hosted by the University of Georgia. There were several other athletic directors, head coaches, and school presidents, most notably Joe Paterno and Bobby Knight. Out of that came the first return to higher academic standards. President Davison later was the first president of the College Football Association.

He was already a big fan when I first met him, and he really savored the success the 1980 team had.

REBUILDING LINDSAY SCOTT

One player who had to be dealt with very carefully before the 1980 season was split end Lindsay Scott. He was outstanding as a freshman in 1978. He ran a kickoff back at LSU to help us win in Baton Rouge. He had already proven that he could play big-time football, but he had run into some trouble the previous offseason.

First, he clashed with one of our academic counselors at the dorm, and I had taken away his scholarship.

John Kasay, who lived at the dorm with the players, characterized the conflict between Scott and academic counselor Curt Fludd as a shoving match.

"They grabbed each other, and both realized that the situation was getting out of hand," John said. "It's an example of how most people never realize that although these college football players all look big and strong and look like men, they aren't. They make mistakes just like kids do."

"It was immaturity on my part," recalled Scott of his conflict with Fludd. "I apologized to him and to the staff and to the team. I had to grow up. Either you follow the rules or you can't be here. I laugh at it now. It was about a girl. The anger and the rage were not toward Fludd. It was about a relationship with a girl. Now it is funny, but then again at the same time, I didn't handle that situation well."

Then, as if coming back from that disciplinary issue was not enough, Scott was in an automobile accident in June that set him back in the early part of the season.

"I had a new car," Scott related. "I had to take it back home to Jesup to get the air conditioning put in. I left about 6 a.m. I was sleepy. It was a fluke accident. I got as far as Soperton, Georgia, and I don't remember anything. I woke up two or three days later in the hospital with my mom and dad there. They told me what happened. I had fallen asleep at the wheel. The car was totaled, and I was ejected. I had a dislocated little toe and a slight concussion."

I present the spring football awards to Lon Buckler (81), a backup receiver; Hugh Nall (54), starting center; Bob Kelly (29), reserve secondary and kicking game specialist; and Robert Miles (83), a tight end who became a defensive end for 1980.

Receivers coach Charles Whittemore felt that Scott was not really full speed until the Florida game.

"I think it affected the coaching staff more than me," Scott countered. "They weren't really sure, was I there or what could I do? They took it slow. I did some therapy. I did take some medication. When I first started running, my equilibrium was off. My balance was off. Once I started running and got back in shape, everything was okay."

EXPECTATIONS VARIED

What were the expectations for 1980? Coaches and athletes are always optimistic, but they are realists, too.

"Every year I expected to do good things," flanker Anthony Arnold said. "My freshman year [1977] we had so many injuries, we could hardly ever put the same team on the field. Then the next year, the public did not have high expectations, but as a team, we did. That was the Year of the Wonderdogs, the underdogs. With the nucleus of that team coming back in 1979, we expected to do well again."

Instead the 1979 team struggled to a 6-5 record. Georgia was 5-1 in the SEC, nearly tying Alabama for the championship, but 1-4 outside of the conference, beating only Georgia Tech. The big difference between the 1978 team that was 9-2-1 and the 1979 team was the void at tailback. Willie McClendon was gone.

"Players have to overcome their coaching," line coach John Kasay added. "Players have to *do* things. A play is only designed to do certain things. You don't expect to go 100 yards on a quarterback sneak. A handoff gets three or four yards, and a sweep may get 10 or 12. In 1979, we didn't have a player who could make something big happen when we handed him the ball, who could take the football and run it 10 or 12 yards up the field."

"Coming out of 1979, with the same players, we expected to have a good team," Arnold added. "Did I look to win all of them? I did that every year. As we progressed through that year, I saw no team that should have beaten us."

NATIONAL CHAMPIONSHIP HOPES?

But realistically, no one was thinking of a national championship in August.

"If we were going to win anything, our goal was the SEC championship," John Kasay said. "To think about a national championship before the first game, you are kidding yourself. You get to a national championship winning mini-goals and stacking them on top of each other.

"We started thinking about a national championship after the Florida game. 'Now you got a chance.' You try to win game after game after game."

"I thought we could be pretty darn good," rover Chris Welton said. "But the one missing piece of the puzzle was running back. We knew it would be tough without a good running back. Matt Simon and Carnie Norris were good running backs but not the kind you could ride to a championship. We thought we could compete for an SEC championship if we got some breaks."

I recall what I wrote in a letter to the team members as we started practice that fall. I wrote, "Our football team possesses all of the ability to be champions. We have a very good football team that could become a great football team, but we must prove that to everyone. Our goal will be to win every game we play and be as good as we can be and to play with an uncontrollable desire to win."

I pointed out that no goals could be reached, no dreams could come true, no miracles could happen unless a person could visualize himself in those situations.

"Begin now to see yourself working hard," I wrote, "to see yourself as part of a total team which is the real secret to our success, and to see yourself with an uncontrollable desire to win, and finally, picture yourself in the winner's locker room."

Chapter Five

TENNESSEE

IT COULD HAVE BEEN A RIVALRY

When Georgia and Tennessee opened the season against each other in 1980, it was only the 18th time the two schools had ever played each other, despite the fact that both universities had been in the same conference for close to 60 years.

Tennessee had its traditional rivals, and we had our traditional rivals, and they did not include each other.

Our traditional games were always with Georgia Tech, Alabama, Auburn, and Florida. Tennessee counted Georgia Tech and Alabama among its big conference rivals.

In the bygone days of the SEC, teams typically played a minimum number of conference games, six or fewer. Georgia, in fact, played only five several times because we lost a conference game with Georgia Tech's secession from the conference. When we shared the conference championship with Alabama in 1966, our 28-3 win over ACC-opponent North Carolina was counted as a conference game. Indeed, there were across the league that year five non-conference games that counted as conference games, including Tennessee's 29-17 win over South Carolina.

Also, when General Bob Neyland was the coach at Tennessee, he was famed for planning his schedule carefully so he never had to play two tough opponents back to back. Georgia against Tennessee would have automatically been a natural rivalry because of the states being adjacent, but the traditional rivalries got in the way.

Shortly after I arrived in 1964, the SEC started working on its first round-robin schedule. In the original format, teams played five regular opponents every year and rotated through the other four opponents with home-and-home series. It took eight years under that format to play every other team in the league home and home.

Georgia's regular opponents were Auburn, Florida, Kentucky, Mississippi, and Vanderbilt. Georgia Tech had dropped out of the SEC by then. Georgia versus Mississippi was about as nontraditional as it could get. Because of the distance between the schools, we had played each other only four times before 1966. But we played each other every year thereafter until 2002 when the SEC schedule underwent another revision.

It would have been much more natural to include Alabama among our traditional opponents, because we had played annually between 1944 and 1966, and our history went back much further than that. But that rivalry had been poisoned by a story published by the *Saturday Evening Post*. The story reported that Alabama coach Paul "Bear" Bryant and Georgia athletic director Wally Butts had conspired to fix the outcome of the 1962 game between the teams. Both Bryant and Butts sued the magazine. Bryant ultimately settled out of court, but Butts won his suit. It became a landmark case in libel law. Ask any college journalism student.

So despite their proximity, despite the fact that Georgia and Tennessee often recruited against each other and despite our membership in the same conference, a game featuring Georgia against Tennessee was quite rare in 1980.

THERE *WAS* A HISTORY, HOWEVER

Although we had seldom played Tennessee, there was still an interesting history between us, especially involving games in Knoxville.

We had opened the season against each other in 1968, a gridiron match, which was fraught with controversy before, during, and after the game.

That was the first time that the schools had played against each other in 31 years. It was also the first game that was played on artificial turf in Neyland Stadium. During the offseason, Tennessee had installed a surface that was branded as Tartan Turf.

Artificial turf was in its infancy. In fact, up to that point, we had played only one game on artificial turf. The previous year we had lost at Houston 15-14 in the Astrodome.

Our athletic director, Joel Eaves, and Bob Woodruff, the Tennessee athletic director, were two ADs who didn't see eye to eye. They used to fuss at each other at some of the AD meetings, and Coach Eaves would get pretty mad.

Well, Coach Eaves was mad when he found out the game was going to be played on this Tartan Turf. Football was supposed to be played on grass, and the contract to play this game was signed with the expectation we would play on grass.

There was so much being written about playing on artificial turf that I tried to downplay it. I remembered when I first came to Georgia, how the players all seemed to wear so much extra armor that they looked like armadillos. I did away with that. People were talking about wearing extra pads for this game, and I reverted back to my first years. I didn't want to see anybody with extra pads on.

As it turned out, it was a mistake. A lot of players had abrasions, and that led to boils and staph infections. On the other hand, we won a conference championship, so maybe it united them as a team.

The game was played on national television. Tennessee was the defending conference champion, and we had been co-champion the year before that. It was a big-time matchup that seemed almost like an intersectional game because of the rarity of previous encounters.

The 1968 game was close, but two big plays put us ahead 17-9 late. Jake Scott had returned a punt 90 yards for a touchdown, and Bruce Kemp had broken off an 80-yard touchdown run.

Sophomore quarterback Mike Cavan made his debut in that game, playing most of the game after coming off the bench to relieve Donnie Hampton.

"I vividly remember that we had come off the field after a score, and it was 17-9," Mike recalled. "We were sitting there on the sideline, and there was not much time, and they were way back. We thought the game was over.

"They moved the ball on us, and all of a sudden we realized that they could score and go for two, so we started pulling for the defense. I think they made two or three fourth-down plays, too.

"I remember their quarterback dropping back on the last play and seeing no time on the clock, and he threw it in the end zone, and they scored."

It was a 30-yard pass down the middle, and the ball hit the ground, but it was ruled a touchdown. And they went for two and tied it.

For Tennessee, the game seemed much more like a win than for us. We could take little solace in the fact that television replays clearly indicated that the touchdown pass was fielded on the bounce.

The controversy did not die that day, however.

The Monday of the following week, WAGA-TV, Channel 5, in Atlanta, interrupted its normal morning programming to announce that the SEC Committee for Fair Play had reviewed films and tapes of the games and reversed the official's call on the touchdown and declared Georgia the winner.

The other Atlanta TV stations had received the same press release, as well as other media outlets. Of course, it was a hoax. The SEC Committee for Fair Play did not exist.

But only Channel 5 had swallowed the hook.

A FORTUITOUS BOUNCE

Our next trip to Knoxville was in 1973, but it did not open the season. Led by senior quarterback Andy Johnson, that team had high expectations that year. We received an early boost when freshman Gene Washington proved adept at returning kickoffs. He returned two for touchdowns against Clemson and North Carolina State.

But the 1973 team hit a major roadblock in Tuscaloosa, Alabama, where Georgia had never won a game and did not until 2002. But we looked like a winner in 1973, leading 14-13 late. Washington had broken his leg earlier in the game and was lost for the season, but we were on the verge of a big win.

But two calls by the officials went in favor of Alabama. First, our punter Don Golden appeared to be roughed when he punted the ball away late in the fourth quarter. But the referee did not throw a flag, and Alabama responded with a quick touchdown drive that put us in a comeback mode.

But the worst call came on a long pass from Johnson to Kevin Hartman that would have put us in scoring position. Game film confirms that Hartman was in-bounds by two steps. But the official, I think influenced by Alabama cheerleaders signaling incomplete, ruled the ball was caught out of bounds. That call haunted that official, who was a car dealer in Atlanta. Sales suffered so much that he had to quit officiating.

We couldn't recover from that call, and Alabama scored another touchdown in the closing seconds to nail down a 28-14 win.

The defeat cut the heart out of that Georgia team. We came back the next week and beat Ole Miss 20-0 before losing consecutively to Vanderbilt 18-14 and Kentucky 12-7, the only time that ever happened while I was coaching at Georgia.

But we somehow found ourselves that day in Knoxville, and we found a freshman linebacker as well. Sylvester Boler of Augusta burst onto the scene in a huge way that day, making 17 tackles, including a decisive stop on a questionable fake punt attempt late in the fourth quarter.

That set us up in good field position. Even when Johnson and Glynn Harrison mishandled a handoff, the ball bounced off Tennessee's artificial turf right into Johnson's hands, and he ran uncontested around end for a clinching touchdown.

Among those most amazed that day was radio announcer Larry Munson, who had mistaken the fumble for a fake handoff. Munson was still early in his career as our announcer, and winning a game in Knoxville was a huge accomplishment for him, considering that he had announced many Vanderbilt defeats there before coming to Athens.

A FAMILIAR FACE ON THE OPPOSITE STAFF

A sidelight to preparing for the Tennessee game in 1980 was that their offensive coordinator, Bill Pace, had been on our staff from 1974 to 1979.

"Bill was a sharp offensive mind," recalled Charlie Whittemore, who was receivers coach under both Pace and his successor, George Haffner.

"He was the type of guy who called plays based on what he saw," Charlie said. "For example, if he looked out there and saw the defense do something, he could think of a play and call it. He was very good at dissecting the other team.

"Bill practiced the same way we played. In other words we would go to practice and he would see whomever we were running against and how they were lined up, and he would call a play. The problem was that those guys might not do the same things on Saturday."

George tended to script practice more and drill plays repeatedly until he was satisfied that the players were prepared to execute those plays, against a variety of defenses and from a variety of offensive sets.

Having drilled against Pace in practice for five years, our defensive coordinator Erk Russell seemed particularly prepared that week.

"That was part of the drama as it unfolded," said Chip Wisdom, Georgia's linebackers coach in 1980. "Not only did we have to go to Tennessee to play against a team that is vastly superior, but it has your former offensive coordinator who has designed everything that he can to beat the defense that he has beaten on the practice field, where he has shared all kinds of confidences with staff members. Bill is a great guy, a great coach, but now he is at Tennessee. So you know he has things ready."

Erk did not change his defensive strategies for the game just because Bill Pace was familiar with us.

"We really had to prepare for them," Chip said, "and Bill knew that. He was going to have some more wrinkles, and he knew how we would probably adjust. He came out with some spread formations and some unique things to see if we would follow our same way of doing things."

The most telling moment of Erk's familiarity with Bill's tendencies came when Tennessee attempted a two-point conversion.

Defensive coaches guess and offensive coaches vice versa. Erk may have had a pretty good sense of what Bill may have run. I thought they were going to run a quick trap up the middle. In Bill's mind, that was where we were vulnerable, because he knew what we did defensively. At that time, we slanted in and stopped them on the two-point play, which was the difference in the game.

ROBERT MILES IS A ...

One of the last personnel moves that Bill Pace inadvertently made while at Georgia was to negotiate a shift of Robert Miles from tight end to defensive end. Aside from having to face Miles in the season opener, a candid comment Bill made turned into a running joke that lasted throughout the season.

As a walk-on, Miles labored to find his place on our football team. In fact, he originally came to Georgia as a walk-on basketball player out of Montgomery, Alabama.

The wife of one of the assistant basketball coaches, Calvin Jones, was one of Miles's neighbors, and that was the connection that brought Miles from Montgomery to Athens. Miles also wanted to be far enough away from home so he wouldn't be home every weekend.

But before he ever dribbled a basketball for Georgia, Miles walked on to the football team, playing on the junior varsity squad under Mike Castronis and Howard "Doc" Ayers. He never made it to basketball. That program was going through a transformation anyway, with Hugh Durham assuming the head-coaching position in 1979, bringing in such all-stars as Dominique Wilkins, James Banks, and Vern Fleming. There was little demand for a six-foot-three forward with average skills.

In the meantime, Miles earned a football scholarship the spring of his freshman year. First he was an understudy to Ulysses Norris and Mark Hodge at tight end. Then in 1979, he started the season as Georgia's No. 1 tight end.

That was the only team I ever had that started out 0-3. On an 0-3 team, Miles was one of the players who lost his starting position as we made adjustments.

"On an 0-3 team, nobody has a job," Miles said.

Miles went from starter to scout team, courtesy of Bill Pace, who was looking to find a winning combination on offense. Miles did not pout, but instead tried to make the best of it, and he put forth a good effort in practice. That impressed Erk Russell. Later Erk negotiated a deal, moving Miles from scout team tight end to reserve defensive end.

"They felt like Robert was not going to get much playing time at tight end," Erk said.

Bill asked Erk if he wanted Miles on defense, and then he added almost as an afterthought: "Robert Miles is a pansy."

Erk took him.

"He was a big ole guy, and apparently he had a good attitude," Erk recalled. "That kind of stuck with me. I might have told Robert when we were changing him to defense, 'Coach Pace said, "You were a pansy," but we are going to give you a chance.'"

All of that took place in 1979. So nearly a year later, the Monday before the Tennessee game, as the defensive players stretched and warmed up, Erk had an idea of how he could use Bill's comment to his favor, not only with Miles, but with the whole team.

Erk always did the calisthenics, and he tried to be funny.

"I tried to make it a fun time," he said, "because the players were about to embark on two hours of misery."

So on the Monday before the Tennessee game, Erk pulled this yellow piece of paper out of his pocket and yelled to the team, "We just got a telegram from coach Bill Pace, the offensive coordinator at the University of Tennessee.

"It says, 'Robert Miles is a pansy!'"

Everybody laughed. Then every week, every Monday, as we got ready for the next opponent, Erk would use the head coach's name, whoever it was: "We just got this telegram."

And every week Robert Miles was the butt of the joke.

"Sometimes," Erk recalled, "you know, I would forget, and one of the players would say, 'What about the telegram?' I'd pull out a piece of paper. 'Charlie Pell says, "Robert Miles is a pansy."'"

"And everybody would laugh, and every game it went that way."

Miles accepted the teasing with a good nature. In fact, like the rest of the players, he looked forward to Erk's joke. It was a ritual that loosened the team up each week.

"It was almost like a unifying thing," Miles said. "Practice had not officially begun until he said it."

"We knew we would hear it on Mondays sometime during our run through," Frank Ros said.

Miles actually had the last laugh before the Sugar Bowl, when before Erk could make his statement, he shouted, "Coach Russell, coach Dan Devine says you are a pansy!"

"It was the Monday before we left Athens," Ros recalled. "It was our first practice, and all of us heard Miles yell, 'Coach Devine says you're a pansy!' We just died, everybody. All of us were on the ground we were laughing so hard. We thought it was the greatest thing we ever heard."

On one level, Miles was tempting fate by twisting the superstition around.

"I didn't think of it as a jinx," he laughed. "It was my turn."

WHO IS PLAYING TAILBACK?

Although Tennessee had not been heavily involved in the recruiting battle for Herschel Walker, there was still a lot of interest in Walker from Knoxville and from all points before the season.

But Walker had done little in the preseason drills to distinguish himself. There was a clamor for news of Walker, but I was trying to keep the pressure off.

In hindsight, it seems ridiculous, but some of the coaches on our staff questioned how effective Walker would be as a college player.

There was no question that Walker was a magnificently gifted athlete, blessed with a rare combination of size and world-class speed. But raw numbers do not always equate to effectiveness on the football field. What was really not known at the time was the super intangibles Walker brought to the game: mental toughness, self-sacrifice, and self-discipline. Combined with his physical talent, those qualities separated him from the rest.

The summer before his senior year in high school, Chip Wisdom remembered him participating in a football camp at Georgia, where the coaches got their best look yet at him, already hyped as a phenomenal prospect.

"We ran him through every position coach to get an opinion of whether they thought the great Herschel Walker would be a top prospect to find out what we thought he could play," Chip recalled,

Georgia's linebackers coach in 1980. "And to be honest with you, not a lot of us thought he could play at our position.

"I certainly didn't think he could play linebacker. We didn't think he could play safety or defensive line, although he could run fast and was big and strong."

His speed would be wasted in the offensive line, and it seemed unlikely he would be a good wide receiver.

"As it later turned out, he really is a great receiver," Chip said. "But in our short time to see him and in our dim-witted vision, none of us saw he could be anything great."

The two positions that seemed most suitable at the time for Walker were tailback and tight end.

"Before you start thinking about him as a tailback, you think a guy like him could be a big blocking fullback," Chip recalled. "There was great enthusiasm to get him, but once we got him, having seen him in camp, we really weren't sure about him."

Walker was third team entering the Tennessee game and had done nothing out of the ordinary in the preseason.

Backfield coach Mike Cavan had a theory that Walker governed his effort in preseason drills in deference to his teammates.

"It was kind of funny," Mike remembered. "Everything as far as coaching him couldn't have been any better. He was always the first one to a meeting. The first time we put a clock on him, it was ridiculous. We had never really had anybody who could run like that.

"But in practice nothing really happened. I really believe that he didn't want to come in here and show up anybody. A couple of things did happen, one in particular.

"We had an Oklahoma drill at the end of two-a-days. The defense was dominating, and it was down to the last one and Herschel got a little frisky. I could always tell. The last one, he pushed the other back aside. I think it was Catfish Jackson who was the defensive lineman. They snapped the ball, and I don't know who the guard was, but he threw him aside, and Herschel hit Catfish. It was like Bill Bates, and he absolutely ran over him.

"Everybody was like, 'What was that? Who was that?' But that was about it. He was okay. You knew it was there. He didn't see any reason to show anybody up at the time. He would do it when the time came. He just didn't have the adrenaline flowing, but when they turned the lights on, there was never a competitor like him."

Mike also understood that I was playing it close to the vest with Walker. He had experienced the same thing when he was Georgia's quarterback in 1968. Though Mike ultimately started and played most of the 1968 season, senior Donnie Hampton started the opener at Tennessee.

Still, Mike lobbied to start Walker at tailback in the season opener.

"Every day the staff would talk about personnel," Mike remembered. "We were getting ready for opening game in 1980, and I made a comment, because I knew how difficult it was for freshmen to start. I could appreciate that there were good reasons, and it was wise in a lot of ways. But I did make the statement that we are not going to be better in 1980 until we tried another tailback."

I told him we were not starting Walker. I appreciated his input, but he would not start. But I had determined that he would play.

"It was really very, very wise," Mike said. "There was no sense in putting that kind of pressure on a guy in the preseason. But it didn't take us but 30 minutes of football to figure out who our tailback was."

SPECIAL SHOES FOR THE PUNTER

Entering the 1980 season, Jim Broadway was our second-team punter behind Mark Malkiewicz, a senior who had paid his dues as a career backup himself.

"I was expecting to travel and to eat steak," Broadway said.

That changed suddenly Tuesday in practice before the Tennessee game. During a full-speed punting drill, freshman Freddie Gilbert blocked one of Malkiewicz's punts.

We had not had enough full-speed kicking under pressure. I can remember it clearly. When Gilbert got his hand on the football, he caught the ball and brought it down on Malkiewicz's foot and flipped him in the air.

Malkiewicz landed awkwardly and broke his collarbone.

Just like that, Broadway became our punter. He doesn't recall being particularly nervous about it, but I was.

"Tuesday to Saturday was a blur," Broadway recalled. "I remember some unusual things. I remember it was the last trip we ever took with those twin-engine planes out of Athens. It took two of them to get us there. I remember flames shooting out of the engines."

In Knoxville itself, Broadway remembers the roads being in disarray while the city prepared for a World's Fair.

But in particular, he remembers his new shoes.

Broadway had coveted a pair of Puma turf shoes like those worn by Mike Garrett, our previous punter. He wanted a pair in the worst way, but Howard Beavers, our equipment manager, never had any turf shoes his size.

Word spread pretty quickly the afternoon that Malkiewicz was hurt and that Broadway was thrust into the starting role.

"Mr. Beavers found those shoes, and he even offered me a different size for each foot if I wanted," Broadway said. "He had been holding out on me."

INSIDE KNOWLEDGE

Back then, we had a practice of going to the visiting stadium the night before the game and going through a light workout. When we were warming up Friday night in Knoxville, somebody found a piece of paper from a yellow pad with a bunch of plays written on it.

It was very much like at the battle of Antietam when the Union army found the Confederate game plan. They discovered the fact that General Lee's army was split. He had sent Stonewall Jackson down to Harper's Ferry, and his army was split in half. If the Union forces had moved then instead of delaying like General McClelland did, things would have been different—so even though he had the game plan, Jackson was able to get back.

That came to my mind, me being a historian and Civil War buff. Erk, of course, was the one who was interested, because it was offensive plays. He and his staff huddled that night and tried to decipher all of that. I think it came out that it was a help to them.

IN THE HEAT OF THE NIGHT

The sweltering heat that had enveloped Georgia throughout August fell on Knoxville that night. It is one of the aspects that practically every player remembers from the game. It was oppressive enough that concession stands ran out of ice by halftime.

"You couldn't hardly breathe," receiver Anthony Arnold said. "You suffocated, and it was night-time!"

"After the game, our fullback, Jimmy Womack, went into body cramps," Frank Ros said. "That game was 120 degrees on the field."

Womack said there were times he wanted to come out of the game because of heat exhaustion, but quarterback Buck Belue knew how to encourage him.

Belue didn't have any magical words, but he looked at Womack and said, "Jimmy, we've got to do this." That was enough.

"It was so hot and humid in there that I sweated out all my body fluids," Womack confirmed.

"That was survival," offensive guard Jim Blakewood said. "It was the hottest game I can ever remember playing. I think they had watered the turf on a hot summer day, and it was almost like a steam rising off of it. We ran 77 plays, and it seems that I ran down about a dozen punts.

"I forget how much weight I lost, but it was ridiculous. When I got back to Athens, I took a chair and just sat in the shower."

"ENJOY THE ATMOSPHERE"

Secondary coach Bill Lewis noticed cornerback Mike Fisher before the game, sitting tensely.

"What's wrong?" Bill asked. "You don't look so good."

"I don't know if you have noticed," Fisher replied, "but we are fixing to go up against three of four members of the world-record holding 400-relay team, Mike Miller, Anthony Hancock, and Willie Gault."

"You know," Bill said. "You have worked at this for all your life. I have you as prepared as you will ever be to play football. Enjoy the atmosphere. Enjoy the ballgame. You will be absolutely fine. Don't worry about any of that stuff."

Looking back on it, Fisher said, "It was like a weight was lifted off my shoulders. He had a way of doing that. He was really connected with his players."

GIVE MY REGARDS TO BROADWAY

Kicking coach Bill Hartman kept a close eye on Jim Broadway as the teams warmed up.

"We desperately tried to get the punter from Jesup who went to Tennessee," said Bill of Tennessee punter John Warren. "I watched them warm up, and that boy from Jesup was kicking it 55, 45, and 65 yards. Broadway was kicking 18 yards and 23 yards. Yet when the game started, that Tennessee boy's first punt was 30 or 32 yards, and Broadway's was 45 or 55 yards."

Credit Bill with an excellent memory. We traded fumbles on our first possessions. Warren's first punt traveled just 32 yards, and his second went 29 yards.

By contrast, Broadway's first punt traveled 51 yards after we stalled on our second possession. He did not have to punt again until early in the second quarter, but this one sliced off the side of his foot, going just 14 yards.

Broadway redeemed himself at the end of the game with a dramatic 47-yard punt out of the Georgia end zone near the end of the game, kicking Tennessee out of field-goal range.

"Broadway won the ballgame just as much as Herschel," Bill said. "He kicked that ball to the Tennessee 43-yard line with no return. If they had made a first down or gotten it on the plus side of the 50, they would have kicked a field goal."

"Everybody remembers the last one," Broadway laughed. "I remember the 14-yarder. They remember the 47-yarder at the end of the game, but they don't remember the 14-yarder that the cheerleader caught. Not only was it not long, it was not high.

"I don't know what happened. Maybe the first one got in my head. I have no idea, other than I probably just looked up."

GOAL-LINE STANDS

Jim Broadway's poor 14-yard punt put Tennessee in excellent field position at our 36 in the second quarter. One of those world-class sprinters, Anthony Hancock, covered most of that distance with a 32-yard reception.

Tennessee had the ball at our four-yard line with a first-and-goal situation. It was to be a recurring theme for the night. Counting the two-point conversion, Tennessee had four possessions inside our five and scored on only one of them.

In the second quarter, they tried four running plays. They gained three yards when they needed four. Whether it was years of experience of competing in practice or plays drawn on a yellow pad, Erk seemed to have us in the right defensive alignment most of the night.

Alas, we did not escape unscathed. For the third time in the game, we fumbled. This time quarterback Buck Belue mishandled the snap, and Jimmy Womack recovered in the end zone for a safety.

Tennessee capitalized on good field position after the free kick as well, driving from its 44-yard line to a touchdown in eight plays.

THE TORCH IS PASSED

Herschel Walker made his first appearance in the game on our first possession after Tennessee's touchdown. I was just waiting to get Walker in the game, waiting to get through my commitment to

Donnie McMickens and Carnie Norris. I was going to give them two drives each and see where we were. Walker was going to get a shot, no question.

His first carry as a Bulldog was a two-yard run up the middle, with Tennessee's White credited with the tackle.

That was Brad White, not Reggie White, another all-time great whose college career started that night. A starter by the end of the year and eventually one of the greatest defensive linemen in the NFL, I do not believe that Reggie White got into the game that night in Knoxville.

Guard Tim Morrison was convinced immediately that Walker was the tailback of the future.

"I remember being in the huddle with Hugh Nall beside me, and I said, 'Hugh, what in the world is Coach Dooley doing?'" Morrison said. "Here comes Herschel running on the field.

"The second play was a 42 Load, and he came straight up my butt, and as I came off the ball, I was steering the linebacker, and the next thing I know he was trying to pull off me to my right. Herschel had stepped into the hole and backed out. He could have gotten about three or four yards. But he backed out and took off around end and got about eight yards. I realized then he was a phenomenal athlete."

WRONG HELMET

Herschel Walker watched the first quarter and a half of the first college game he suited up for, shocked that he was not in the game.

"I thought I was going to play," Walker said. "I thought that's why they recruited me, to play football. So I was shocked when I was told I was not ready. I was totally shocked. Coach Dooley was telling me right before the game I wasn't even going to play."

It's funny what players remember, because I told him he would not start, not that he would not play.

Walker had a similar experience as a sophomore in high school at Johnson County when he was a fullback.

"They had a senior tailback," Walker recalled. "The coaches never really gave me a shot at playing tailback. One game I remember the senior got hurt, and they moved me to tailback. I played only two and a half quarters, and I had maybe five touchdowns and 200 and something yards. I assumed they were going to let me play tailback, but no, they moved me back to fullback."

For us, however, Walker had done little in his first preseason drills to distinguish himself from our other backs. That was why he was third on the depth chart.

Then when I did summon him to play, he was not ready. He couldn't find his helmet. That would cost him $100 years later.

Walker was playing professionally with Jason Sehorn, who one day made a remark about a certain type of helmet that Walker had worn at one time.

Walker denied that he had ever before worn such a helmet. A friendly disagreement resulted, and Sehorn bet Walker $100 that he had indeed worn that type of helmet.

"I wasn't going to bet anything," Walker said, "because I don't like to lose. But I figured I knew what I had worn."

Walker was surprised and $100 poorer when Sehorn showed up with a photo of Walker wearing the disputed helmet in the 1980 Tennessee game.

"I was so shocked and surprised, that I just grabbed somebody's helmet and went in," Walker recalled. "I reckon somebody took a picture with me wearing that helmet, so he ended up winning the bet."

Walker said he remembered too late his mother's words of wisdom: "Never bet on anything."

GOING PLACES

Herschel Walker's statistics were unimpressive at halftime of his first game, but I had seen enough of him to determine that he should carry the load in the second half.

That was when I said, "He may not know where he is going, but he was going somewhere in a hurry." Based on those two drives, I made the decision to start him in the second half.

I did not immediately announce this when we got together at halftime to talk about things, so backfield coach Mike Cavan did not automatically assume that Walker would be inserted into the second-half starting lineup. I wanted the staff to be involved in making decisions.

In the offensive meeting, Mike told George Haffner, "We have to play this guy. He had played in the first half, and he had given us a little spark."

George said, "You are 100 percent right. Go tell Coach Dooley."

"Me! You go tell him! You are the one getting the big bucks!" Mike responded.

But Mike came to me. He didn't mind a challenge. But he was very apprehensive.

"Coach, we've got to play Herschel," Mike said.

"That's fine; that's fine; go ahead," I said.

Of course, we were down 9-0, and I had already decided that he was going to start the second half.

THINGS GET WORSE BEFORE THEY GET BETTER

Even though Herschel Walker had given us a little spurt, his half-time statistics were very ordinary. He had run the ball five times for 18 yards and caught one pass for nine yards.

Walker was not much of a factor early in the third quarter, either. On our first possession, he lost a net three yards in four carries. Buck Belue completed a 13-yard pass to Anthony Arnold and a 27-yard pass to Norris Brown, but the drive stalled.

Our next opportunity fared even worse. Walker gained just a yard on a play that was erased by illegal procedure.

After we punted again, Tennessee struck quickly with a 52-yard, two-play drive. Their quarterback, Jeff Olszewski, completed two passes to Mike Miller, the second one being a 36-yard touchdown.

The stadium noise was a problem all night. It got real loud then.

"I remember the noise factor," safety Jeff Hipp said. "On the field, even in the huddle, it was difficult to hear the plays being called. Frank Ros was calling the defensive plays, and you would have to get in his face to understand what was being called. He always spoke so fast that you had to pick up what you could."

THE TWO-POINT DECISION

The subplot that pitted Tennessee offensive coordinator Bill Pace against his former team came to a climax after Tennessee's second touchdown.

Leading 15-0 with 3:19 to go in the third quarter, Tennessee coach Johnny Majors elected to go for two. Did we have inside knowledge of what play Bill would run?

Erk Russell did not know what play Bill would call.

"It wasn't a play that Erk knew," Chip Wisdom said. "Erk called an all-out blitz, and somehow we got lucky and stopped them."

Tennessee also was flagged for illegal procedure, but naturally we declined the penalty.

Why did Tennessee go for two points, leading by 15?

"Coaches have a chart they rely on of when they should go for two points," Chip explained.

Holding a 15-0 lead in the third quarter is probably not on that chart, yet Tennessee did indeed go for two after its second touchdown.

"Why did they go for two?" Chip asked. "Our two-point chart didn't call for it when you are ahead by that much at that point in the game. Why go for two to hit some magic number? As it was, they lost one by not making the two."

THE MOMENTUM SWINGS

Our next possession was a three-and-out, which seems an unlikely place for a comeback to begin, but on Jim Broadway's punt, Bill Bates muffed the catch.

One of our centers, Joe Happe, was partly responsible. Happe had broken his hand early, but he was still in on the punt team.

"Bates was returning the punt, and I could tell that he was looking straight ahead and that he didn't see me," Happe said. "So as he caught it, I nailed him, and the ball went flying. People were falling all over each other to get on the ball."

That ball must have rolled 20 yards before it went out of the end zone. I think every player on the field had a shot at it at one time or another.

That is one of Larry Munson's great calls. To me it is one of the best ever. The ball kept fumbling, and he kept talking. "Get on that ball!" Somebody would jump on the ball, and it would spurt out and spurt out. It went a long way. I don't know how far it went, but that ball rolled a heck of a long way. There were two or three times where somebody seemed like they had it when it was pushed farther back and Munson was describing it. It was a classic.

The ball bounced all the way through the end zone for a safety.

LINDSAY SCOTT'S FORGOTTEN MOMENT

After Scott Woerner returned the free kick 18 yards to the 50-yard line, we started to move the ball. The drive would end in one of the most famous touchdowns in Georgia football history, Herschel Walker's run over safety Bill Bates.

But forgotten is the previous play, a 24-yard pass play from Buck Belue to Lindsay Scott.

Scott also broke a tackle in a preview of what was to come.

"I knew we had to do something," Scott said. "It was discouraging. But it seemed we got a spark, and the defense shut Tennessee down."

On a bootleg, Belue threw to Scott.

"I didn't do a Herschel," Scott laughed, "but it was one of those plays where the guy tried to tackle me, and I kind of ran over him. But then the next play, Walker... it was like they shot him out of a cannon."

WALKER MEETS BILL BATES

Although the game was not televised, Walker's first touchdown is one of the most familiar plays in Georgia football history. It is included in the highlights from history that are shown before games on the giant screen at Sanford Stadium.

It was a 16-yard run, and Walker ran over Tennessee's safety, Bill Bates, to score. It looks on film like Bates was braced for impact, but I don't think he took Walker seriously. That was true throughout his freshman year. People just tried to lean over and tackle him high. After a while they learned. You better be braced for the tackle, and you better come in low. The next year his yards were tougher because they came at him lower and en masse.

Walker's run was so awe-inspiring that Georgia announcer Larry Munson exclaimed, "My God! He's running over people!"

Walker and Bates were later teammates with the Dallas Cowboys.

"Bill and I never talked about it," Walker said. "Everybody else talked about it. That is all people ever, ever talked about. I felt bad about it for Bill."

Walker still defends Bates.

"If you look at the film, first of all, he slipped," Walker said. "As he was coming up, he lowered his head, and that is when I hit him. Bill is an excellent tackler, a tough, tough guy. I felt bad, because it was not fair for them to show that film all the time. He turned out to be one of the toughest guys I had ever played with."

"Bill was just not ready," guard Tim Morrison agreed. "When you get ready to tackle Herschel, you have to be ready to take on a machine running at you."

Many of the players in the game didn't even see the play. The game remains one of left tackle Jeff Harper's most memorable of his college experience, simply because both of Walker's touchdowns were run behind him at left tackle. But Harper didn't see the results until the following day in the film room.

"You never see the play, because you are taught to stay on your man until the whistle blows," Harper said. "You can't look back and see who is coming your way."

Wide receiver Lindsay Scott, who was a few yards away blocking at the time, saw it.

"It was a showdown in the middle of the field," he said.

"I was as surprised as anyone by Herschel when we got up to Knoxville," rover Chris Welton remembered. "When you hit him in practice, you felt the power, the strength. You thought physically he was gifted. But in summer camp I never saw him turn it on. As I recall, I was standing next to Frank Ros when he ran over Bill Bates. It was electrifying. We just looked at each other. The feeling was, 'Let's go play defense and get the ball back, so he can do that again.' It was like someone put a current of electricity through us."

Cornerback Greg Bell recalled the play as the first time Walker used the leverage of his shoulders and thighs properly.

"It wasn't until Bill Bates, that play, where he got his shoulders down for the first time. Of course, he had huge shoulders and a small waist, and after that, nobody wanted to touch him. He had found his strength."

Flanker Anthony Arnold remembers the play, and he inadvertently contributed to one of the most legendary plays in Georgia's history.

"I should have been helping out on that play," Arnold laughed. "I didn't go block. As a wide receiver, it was your job to run get the safety man. I didn't get there. [Bates] was one of the guys I was supposed to block. If I had been hustling...."

Walker might have scored anyway, but it would have been much less memorable, and Bates would not have been such a prominent footnote in Georgia's march to the national championship.

ONE MORE GOAL-LINE STAND

Turnovers would prove to be a major part of our success in 1980, and Tennessee fumbled it right back to us two plays after the kickoff. We started at the Tennessee 37-yard line, and we ended with another touchdown run by Herschel Walker, this one for nine yards around the left end. We kicked the extra point, and we were up 16-15.

Nate Taylor was ready to make a play.

But Tennessee made one more try to go ahead. They completed a couple of big pass plays, and with less than five minutes to go they had another first and goal at our five-yard line. All they needed was a field goal. That was the worst thing that could happen to them.

But really, that was *not* the worst that could happen to them.

THE TACKLING MACHINE

Herschel Walker's exploits notwithstanding, we might not have beaten Tennessee were it not for the play of an unlikely hero.

Linebacker Nate Taylor came to Georgia as unheralded as any high school player. Yet he was ready when fate intervened, and as a result made a critical play to save the win over Tennessee.

"'Ty Ty' was just a phenomenal tackling machine," said 1980 line-backers coach Chip Wisdom, calling Taylor by his nickname. His hometown was a wide spot in the road near Tifton, Georgia.

"He would always end up making a tackle, or he would cause a fumble or do something," Chip recalled. "How does this guy do that? You don't know how. You just know he does, so you play him."

Taylor made one of those plays late against Tennessee.

There was 11:16 still remaining when Georgia went ahead. We traded punts, with Tennessee gaining the edge in field position, primarily because of a 67-yard punt by John Warren. With 6:59 to play, they started a drive from the Tennessee 41, and it had all the markings of a game-winning drive.

They completed a couple of big pass plays and made a couple of good runs, and all of a sudden they had a first-and-goal at the Georgia five-yard line with the clock nearing the four-minute mark.

For the third time in the game, Tennessee found itself with a first-and-goal inside the five. But on their third deep probe, running back Glenn Ford met Taylor personally. Taylor's hit forced a fumble, and defensive end Pat McShea recovered on the Georgia two-yard line. Counting a stand on Tennessee's failed two-point try in the third quarter, we stopped the Volunteers three of four times inside our own five-yard line.

Taylor played for Tift County High School, but he was not widely recruited by colleges. In fact, Vanderbilt turned him down even as a walk-on.

Taylor walked on at Georgia, where the coaches discovered the full limit of his measurable abilities.

"As I remember, he had little, slow feet," Chip said. "He could waddle better than anybody I ever saw.

"He couldn't run fast. He ran a 5.3 40. I don't think Nate ever broke five-flat. I'm exaggerating obviously, but he was slow."

Despite his sluggishness afoot, he excelled in games.

"Nate could sort of waddle around and avoid blocks and end up making tackles," Chip explained. "He never had to bend his knees, because he was so much shorter than the running backs. He was a shrimp. He weighed 193 pounds. Yet he was the leading tackler [in 1979]."

"He was the kind of guy who I don't think you would go back and see him play in high school twice," Erk Russell remembered. "Yet when you turned him loose, he seemed to know where the ball was. He had a Tasmanian devil-type disposition."

Offensive line coach Wayne McDuffie was the first to notice Taylor, when he was still relegated to the scout team that practiced against the varsity lineup each day.

"Wayne kept saying, 'Chip, you get that little son of a bitch on your defensive team! He is screwing up our offensive practice every damn day!' Chip said. "He would go full speed and make tackles and make the offensive linemen look bad."

Still, Taylor remained on the scout team, where he might have languished had fate not intervened.

In 1979, searching for solutions, we had moved Jimmy Payne, an all-star defensive tackle, to linebacker.

"That was a big mistake," Chip opined, "to take an All-American out of one position and to make him a hurt, injured player at another position."

It was early in the 1979 season, the third game, against South Carolina, when Payne was injured.

"When Jimmy goes down and limps off the field and the pit of your stomach is empty because you realize what a loss he is going to be, I couldn't find anybody else to put in the game, except Nate," Chip explained.

"I forget who the scholarship second-team linebacker was, it's not important, but I couldn't find him. And Nate, even though he was a scout-team player, he wasn't supposed to be playing.

"But I ran him in, and he makes a tackle on George Rogers, who won the Heisman Trophy the next year. I'm dumb, but I'm not stupid. I'm not taking him out until he screws up. Well, he doesn't screw up, so we leave him in the rest of the game, and he makes about 18 tackles."

Taylor started every game the rest of his Georgia career and received a scholarship the following week.

"He got that battlefield scholarship because he was ready, and half of being in the right place at the right time is being ready," Chip said, "Man, if there was ever a great example of why you should be ready as a football player or an athlete or anybody on the sidelines looking for a chance … he was looking for a chance, and he caught one."

THE GREATEST FUMBLE RECOVERY IN GEORGIA HISTORY

Pat McShea likes to joke that he made "the greatest fumble recovery in the history of Georgia football."

"If they don't fumble …" McShea pointed out. "We had a lot of luck that year. You change four plays, and we are 7-4."

McShea remembers the play clearly.

"They ran the lead play," he said. "We ran a middle blitz, and Nate [Taylor] shot in there and hit him, helmet on the ball, and the ball popped back. I was folding back. I was supposed to be coming up field. But I saw the ball and fell on it.

"There was a huge pileup," McShea said. "One Tennessee player grabs my throat and starts squeezing while another one tried to pull the ball away. I took my facemask and pressed down on his

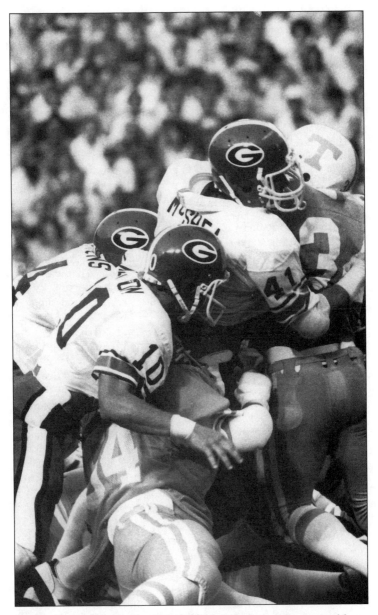

Joe Creamons, Pat McShea (41), and Chris Welton (10) gang-tackle a Tennessee player in 1980. McShea recovered a fumble late in the game to preserve Georgia's 16-15 win.

wrist, down on the Astroturf, until he let go of my throat. And finally, it seemed like forever, I was able to get up, and we had the ball."

ONE MORE BULLET TO DODGE

There were still just over four minutes to play in the game when we took over at our own two-yard line. Herschel Walker ran three times, but a delay-of-game penalty and Tennessee's desperate defense forced a fourth-and-six from the Georgia six-yard line.

Jim Broadway would have to punt one more time.

"We all thought Tennessee was going to score before the fumble," Broadway said. "Then after they fumbled, it seemed like we ran three of the fastest plays I can remember. I didn't even contemplate going into the game. I can still visualize the ball on the left hash mark and my foot being about a yard away from the back of the end zone. And for some reason, they did not call a timeout."

"When we didn't move the ball too well," McShea said, "that meant Broadway had to kick it out of the end zone. That was when everyone was really nervous. Everyone knows his personality. He was not going to be able to handle the pressure, and then he boomed a 47-yarder."

I don't ever recall in my 25 years as head coach being more uptight than I was at that moment, watching Broadway stand deep in the end zone waiting for the snap that could determine the outcome. Boy, was I relieved when I saw that ball sail high and deep out of the end zone!

That meant Tennessee had to make a couple of first downs most likely before they could kick a field goal. We blitzed on four straight plays, climaxed by Jimmy Payne's sack of Jeff Olszewski that finally clinched the win.

"I was talking to Bill Lewis after the game," Broadway recalled. "It didn't strike me how important the kick was until after the game, getting on the plane. I got a little shaky about it then."

THE GAME THAT SET THE TREND

There was still an entire season to be played, but the way we played in that first win gave us a confidence that would stay with us the rest of the year. Whenever we found ourselves in a tough spot, we had a reservoir of confidence to draw on.

"It all emanated from the Tennessee game," punter Jim Broadway said. "After that game, we didn't think we were going to lose."

"Tennessee was probably the best team we played by far," linebacker Frank Ros said. "Later on they got beat by Southern Cal on a last-second field goal, and the same thing happened against Alabama. They got some kids hurt, too. But if we don't win that game, then I'm not wearing a championship ring."

Tennessee did indeed lose a close game to Southern Cal the following week 20-17. Alabama actually beat the Volunteers 27-0, but they did have a close 16-13 loss to Virginia. Eventually defensive lineman Reggie White became a starter.

But only one freshman became a star that hot night in Knoxville, Tennessee.

Chapter Six

TEXAS A&M

PROBLEM SOLVED, PROBLEM CREATED

I n discovering that freshman Herschel Walker could play tail-back, it was obvious that we had found someone we could depend on. But it did create a problem in what to do about Donnie McMickens.

McMickens was a senior who had played sparingly as a running back before 1980. He had started the Tennessee game and played the first two series, but it was obvious from the game that Walker was a much better tailback.

Center Hugh Nall, who became a coach after his playing days, often credited McMickens as the consummate team player.

"He became our best special teams player," Nall said, who liked to cite McMickens's positive response to being benched by Walker.

But the inside story is a little more complicated.

McMickens *did* become a problem after the Tennessee game, but it was a problem that I feel good about, because he was able to address it.

He was a fifth-year senior and had worked all this time to be a starter. He was a good football player.

He started the Tennessee game, which was what he had dreamed of. But by the end of the first half, he no longer had the job. He was beaten out.

When he came back to practice Monday, Donnie McMickens's jaw was down on the ground. He was not good for himself or good for us with his current attitude.

Some of the coaches were concerned that with the newfound Walker, we couldn't have McMickens on the team. "He is ruining the morale of the team," was the general consensus of the coaches.

I do remember this, and I don't like to take credit too often, but I felt good asking the staff, "Let's just hold off a little. Here is a guy who has been here all this time, and he has some ability. He could really help us. Let me talk to him first."

So I did talk to him. I asked him to come into my office. Here's what I told him.

"Donnie, first of all, you have got to own up to certain facts," I said, "and the fact is, you have been beaten out at your position for starting tailback. But on the other hand, you have not been beaten out by any normal human. You have been beaten out by a truly great football player.

"You have to accept that, whether you like it or not. He is a better player.

"On the other hand, in order for us to do what we want to do, we need you on this football team. If you are willing to do it, we want you to be a starter on every special team we have. We need you. We really do."

He bought into it, and he got over that attitude—his lip had been down to the ground. He ended up being captain of the special teams and most valuable special teams player. I don't believe we would have won the national championship without him.

LINE SHUFFLE

Georgia won at Tennessee, but at least three of the assistant coaches went straight to work on their return to Athens in trying to strengthen the team.

"We knew we were lucky as hell to come out of there," recalled John Kasay, the assistant offensive line coach. "We should have lost the game. Herschel saved our cans. He came out of the woodwork. Then they fumbled on the two-yard line going in. Our season could have been drastically affected by six feet.

"Wayne McDuffie and Rusty Russell and I were distraught. We felt like we had a pretty good team, but something was not right. There were times that I was positive about things, but it was not at the beginning of 1980. Of course, I felt good about 1981 and 1982, but you have to remember how much we had struggled in 1979.

"We got back in Athens at 3 a.m., and the adrenaline was still flowing. After being up all day and the emotional drain of football, I used to tell people that I could smell grease coming out of me. Remember, it was hot as hell in Knoxville. I had changed my shirt at halftime. My shirt was soaked through just like I had walked into a shower."

John, Wayne, and Rusty went to the office at 3 a.m., searching for something.

"We were watching the first-half film that they had already sent, and when we reviewed it, we came to the conclusion that our line-up was not proper. We did not have the right people in the right places. Wayne asked me if I had any ideas.

"I was always a third-and-two or a fourth-and-one coach," John stated. "I wanted our offense set up so that if we needed one yard, we could get it. I was not sure that our team could gain a yard on fourth down or two yards on third down.

"Rusty and I had already talked about moving Tim Morrison to right guard and Nat Hudson to right tackle. We had three centers, Wayne Radloff, Joe Happe, and Hugh Nall, all of whom could play that position. We felt like with that lineup we had the people across the line that we could line up and get a first down.

"But who was going to tell Coach Dooley?

"So the next afternoon we were in the staff meeting and discussing how people played. Coach Dooley always wanted a rundown. So Vince asked if anybody had any suggestions, and Wayne, who was always macho as hell, said, 'John has got something to tell you.' That SOB hung me out to dry.

"I wish he had told me he was going to do that. The thing you had to do with Vince was to anticipate what he was going to say, because he was smart.

"See, Nat was having difficulty with adjustments," John continued. "The guard had to be the guy who was telling other people what to do, and Nat was not that kind of guy. He was good at getting his tail in the right place. He was a damn fine blocker. When I look back at his physicality, he is a guy who could play today. He was *strong*. He had so much power, and he did things effortlessly. The first day he walked on the practice field he ran a mile in 5:20. He had a heart like a hummingbird.

"Morrison, on the other hand, was smart, ambitious. I always liked ambitious players.

"So I was trying to gather myself, and I went through the whole scenario and ended by saying that we would be better if we moved Nat from left guard to right tackle.

"And Coach Dooley looked at me, and said, 'You mean to tell me that you are going to teach Nat Hudson to play tackle in one week when you haven't been able to teach him to play guard in four years?'

"I have never been asked a question that I did not have an answer for, but the man was totally and unequivocally correct.

"So I told him that I would do whatever was necessary. So we went that night and stayed up until 4 a.m. making a playbook of just what the right tackle has to do. We put it together and simplified the rules. I think that move we made, that line was what made us the team we were. Now we had the best running offensive linemen in the right spot."

THE SILVER BRITCHES RETURN

The Texas A&M game was the first time Georgia had worn silver britches since the 1963 season, the year before I came to Georgia.

I made some dramatic changes in the uniform when I became the head coach. Georgia had worn silver helmets with a block G and silver pants. The biggest thing I changed was the headgear. But I also changed the pants, partly because I didn't like one of the cheers that was popular then.

They would shout, "Go, you silver britches!" The spirited Georgia students would translate that to "Go, you sons-a-...!" I thought it was inappropriate and not in keeping with the type of program we wanted to build in Georgia.

Of course, by 1980, it was a totally different group of fans cheering, so I felt we could bring back some tradition with the silver pants.

As the season developed, the success we had was the undoing of the red pants, which we wore only for the Tennessee game.

The change with the headgear was more important. I wanted a forward-looking type of emblem, different than the block G. I also thought we had the three greatest colors: black on white on red. Someone described them to me as the most harmonious colors in existence.

I discussed with the staff that a forward-looking G would be an appropriate emblem for the helmet of the Georgia team. One of the coaches I had brought onto the staff was backfield coach John Donaldson, who played at Georgia from 1945 to 1948. John was keen on the idea of a new image and volunteered his wife, Anne, to design a logo for the new Georgia helmet. She was well qualified because she had a bachelor's degree in commercial art from Georgia.

Starting with the general specifications I outlined, Anne designed an original oval G, which fit the vision I had for a forward look to

Georgia's new emblem. Then John and I had people go in the Coliseum and put the headgear on, and in the stadium, and it didn't matter how far away you were, you could see that G stick out because of the harmony of black on white on red.

The Georgia oval G Anne designed was different in design and color from the G used by the Green Bay Packers, but it was similar enough that I thought it best to clear its use with the NFL team. Joel Eaves contacted the Packers, who granted permission.

The Green Bay G was introduced in 1961, and it has been redesigned several times, and now it looks like our original Georgia G. Of course, we are proud of the fact that the Packers apparently liked the special nuances of the Bulldogs' forward-looking G.

The oval Georgia G has stood the test of time, eventually replacing the old block G. It was an immediate hit with the fans and has never lost its appeal. The fact that our program got off to such a great start those first three seasons, highlighted by the 1966 Southern Conference championship, helped gain the acceptance of Georgia fans. It has clearly stood the test of time.

INSIDE KNOWLEDGE

With Herschel Walker firmly entrenched as the starting tailback, just one game into his career, we could turn to our home opener with the confidence that we had supplied one of the missing links from the previous year. Our home opener was against Texas A&M, which certainly was not a traditional rival.

Back in those days, we were able to attract teams on a one-time basis to come to Athens. We have a long history of bringing in teams like Oregon State, Baylor, Pittsburgh, California, North Carolina State, and Virginia. Texas A&M was one of those schools. You could not do that today with any of those schools, but you could do it then. It would help fill our schedule, and it was a name opponent. And it would give us a home game that we would not have to return.

Like us, Texas A&M was coming off a mediocre season, but also like us, they had finished strong. They had won four of their last five games, including a win over archrival Texas the previous year.

And for this game, we would have the advantage of "inside knowledge," because our offensive coordinator, George Haffner, had been on their staff the previous year.

"I went over to Texas A&M in 1979 to join Tom Wilson, their new head coach," George said. "They were breaking from the Wishbone system, and it was a great opportunity.

"Of course, I knew most of the kids at A&M. I'm sure it was something we talked about to the defensive coaches. I had the scouting report because of my experience there the year before."

The Real Inside Tip

While George Haffner's familiarity may have played some role in Georgia's ultimate success against Texas A&M, it was something that defensive coordinator Erk Russell noticed on film that really made a difference.

"Coach Russell had noticed on film that their left tackle gave the play away by his stance," Pat McShea said. "If both his feet were flat, it was going to be pass, unless it was a draw. On a run play, he was in the habit of getting his heel off the ground. My job was to read the stance and signal the secondary."

Cornerback Mike Fisher said that McShea signaled every play with his hands.

"If you go back and look at the film, when they ran the option, you could see our corners come up on the pitch man," McShea explained. "Texas A&M never had a chance."

Whether it was inside knowledge or not, McShea does not remember, but the Aggies fumbled on their second play of the game, and McShea recovered, setting us up in excellent field position. In fairly short order, we were in the end zone, courtesy of a six-yard touchdown pass from quarterback Buck Belue to flanker Anthony Arnold.

Passing, on the Field, in the Classroom

We scored three touchdowns in the second quarter. But instead of relying on Herschel Walker, our passing game accounted for most of the yards.

First, Buck Belue passed to tight end Norris Brown for 53 yards to set up a one-yard score by Walker. Then Belue and Anthony Arnold connected on another 19-yard scoring pass, after two more long pass plays.

And at the end of the half, our backup quarterback, Jeff Paulk, led a 68-yard scoring drive with a 16-yard completion to tight end Guy Stargell, a 23-yard completion to split end Charles Junior, and a 24-yard scoring pass to Chuck Jones with just seven seconds to play in the half.

As it developed, scoring at the end of the half would be a trend that would be repeated several more times during the season.

We had pegged John Lastinger to be the backup quarterback to Buck Belue, but he injured his knee in practice and was lost for the year. Paulk was an outstanding young man and went on to fly with the Air Force Thunderbirds.

Jones was a solid player for us, a fine possession receiver. I remember when he came to see me about helping him get his degree.

When we built the Butts-Mehre Heritage Hall, we put up some signs with motivational messages on it. The first sign as you walk into the first floor from the parking lot showed a football player in uniform and the same player in cap and gown, representing success on the field and in the classroom. The statement underneath read, "If it is to be, it is up to me."

We were supposed to change those signs from time to time, but I liked that one so much that I never changed it.

Jones came in to see me asking for more help as he finished his eligibility.

"Coach, receiving my degree is important to me," he said.

And I replied, "If... , it ... "

He finished the sentence, "If it is to be, it is up to me."

Jones did indeed earn his degree and became a teacher in the Atlanta school system.

I am very pleased that although coach Mark Richt modernized the pictures along the players' walkway in the Butts-Mehre Heritage Hall, he did not change the theme. "If it is to be, it is up to me" is still there today.

Walker scored a second touchdown in the third quarter, this one set up by a 68-yard punt return by Scott Woerner to the Aggie four-yard line.

WALKER SHOWS HIS SPEED

Against Tennessee, Herschel Walker had certainly demonstrated his power, but it was not until the Texas A&M game that the Bulldog Nation got a glimpse of his speed.

When I think of Texas A&M, the first thing that comes to mind is Walker's run at the end of the game. He cinched it, and the crowd really liked it. When Walker got the ball, they were beginning to anticipate something big might happen.

Herschel Walker displayed what he could do on the gridiron against Texas A&M. *Photo by Richard Fowlkes*

The play was Fly 42, and Walker went 76 yards for the touchdown. After Rex Robinson's sixth extra point of the day, it was 42-0 with a quarter to go.

Erk Russell turned to Mike Cavan after Walker's long run and said, "I have been here for 18 years, and I have seen them run by us like that. But we have never had anybody who could do that."

We had seen Walker's speed in time trials and sprints, but this was the first time he had put it on display in a game.

"I realized he could take the ball the distance," tackle Jeff Harper said. "Up until that point, other than Willie McClendon my sophomore year, we did not have a person who if he got into the backfield could go all the way.

"It shouldn't give you any more incentive and confidence, because you should be giving 100 percent every play. But you know subconsciously this is a team. If each individual does what he is supposed to do, then things will fall together."

CONFIDENCE BUILDS

The combination of a close win over a conference rival and a rout of a respected team helped the 1980 team build confidence early in the season.

"In retrospect, after the Tennessee game we thought Herschel Walker was the missing piece," rover Chris Welton said. "Then when Texas A&M came to town the next week, they were expected to be good, and we reamed them. We started thinking that we had a chance to be pretty good."

Secondary coach Bill Lewis saw it, too.

"I will never forget the feeling on the sideline," Bill recalled. "If we took care of business, we could beat anybody. That developed from those two early games. That is important for a team.

"We knew we had a good offensive line of scrimmage, a good solid quarterback with Buck Belue, and we had some weapons. All of a sudden we had that special guy at tailback. Everybody knew that we wanted to run the ball, and the guy who was needed to do that was there. Texas A&M could not catch him. He ran away from them.

"On top of that fourth-quarter win at Knoxville, it set the tone. We were working with a confident team that got better each week."

RELAXED ON THE SIDELINE

At least one member of our coaching staff was not overly impressed with Texas A&M, which finished the year 4-7, but did beat rival Texas again.

John Kasay used to tease me that I needed to do a better job of picking those teams to come in to play us. He said they always seemed to be strong. Baylor came in with Mike Singletary. Pittsburgh brought Tony Dorsett. Brigham Young had Steve Young. California brought in Wesley Walker.

"Coach, you have to do better," John would say with a laugh.

"But Texas A&M ... I don't ever remember being in a football game where I was so relaxed. There were several series of downs where they didn't even gain a yard. After about the fifth series, they come back with the quick stats, and they don't have a yard!"

Chapter Seven

CLEMSON

A Painful Lesson:
Don't Act in Anger

The first game I ever coached in Sanford Stadium was against Clemson. We won 19-7. That was after opening with three games on the road, at Alabama, Vanderbilt, and South Carolina, and I experienced everything a coach could experience: a loss, a win, and a tie. Dan Reeves, by the way, was the quarterback of that South Carolina team.

We played Clemson almost every year. Before we got the round-robin schedule in the SEC arranged, the Clemson game sometimes even counted as a conference game after we were left with too few games when Georgia Tech had dropped out of the conference. I guess they could have counted the Tech game as a conference game, but the SEC was mad at Tech.

We beat Clemson every year until 1974 when we had a snapper snap one over the punter and we stepped out of bounds on our one-yard line on a kickoff return. But those great Junkyard Dog teams of 1975 and 1976 won decisively, 35-7 and 41-0.

But they came to Athens in 1977 and beat us 7-6. We scored late and went for two even after a penalty. I probably shouldn't have done that. I was so mad because we had played so badly. It was one of those games where my emotions got in the way of good judgment.

I was also mad that we got penalized. You never see a penalty on an extra-point play. Those were ACC officials, and they penalized us as we were lining up going for two. That only added to my irritation. I think we threw to Pay Norris over in the corner.

What Might Have Been Avoided

Mike Cavan, who played quarterback for Georgia in the late 1960s, was on the Georgia staff in 1977, and he had responsibility for scouting Clemson.

"When I came on the staff, Clemson was given to me. Each coach on the team had a team they were responsible for. It was not as sophisticated as it is today. I was the new guy, and Clemson was not very good. But I could see that they were getting better and better. I knew going into 1977 that these guys were good.

"We didn't score until late, and we were going for two when we got a delay of game. We still went for two! There are not too many plays you will make eight yards on. We should have kicked the extra point and got out of there, but Coach Dooley was just so mad that we were even in that situation.

"The whole point was Vince never would have had a losing season if we had kicked the extra point. But he was so damn mad at the fact that this was *Clemson*. He was not going to tie the Clemson game. For him that was very unusual. That was out of the box for him. That was one time emotion overtook him.

"From that point on, the Clemson game became an absolute war. It went on year after year."

My teams were 10-1 against Clemson before 1977. I was 5-5-1 against Clemson between 1977 and my retirement in 1988.

The 7-6 decision in 1977 was a watershed event for the Clemson program, which had endured losing seasons eight of the nine previous years. But that 1977 team finished 8-3-1, and the Tigers would not have another losing season for 15 more years.

A footnote to Georgia's failed two-point try: Clemson had only 10 players on the field. That just makes me mad all over again!

Paying the Price

Frank Ros, the captain of the 1980 team, was only on the kick-off team in that 7-6 loss to Clemson, but the loss was costly as he discovered the downside of teamwork.

"Coach was furious after that game," Ros said. "That Sunday morning everybody got a knock on the door at 8 a.m. Coach was so ticked that everybody was coming out to practice. The freshmen had to go against the varsity because he was ticked at them, and it was a big-time battle. We practiced like mad."

It became a football marathon for the freshmen, who left practice with just enough time to change t-shirts, pick up their game jersey, and gobble a sandwich en route to the stadium for the appointed game against South Carolina's freshmen.

"They'd never do that now," Ros said.

WOERNER THE RETURNER

Scott Woerner was the whole game in 1980.

Clemson knocked us all over the field. They just ran up and down the field, and we would make a play. Really, Woerner would make a play.

What most people forget is that Woerner, who was an All-America cornerback for us that year, did not start the Clemson game.

"I started the game," cornerback Greg Bell said. "I graded higher the week before against Texas A&M. I graded 93 percent, and he graded 85 percent. But he could make the big plays.

"Woerner had been kind of putzing around. He had a lot of ability. We had played about equal time at Tennessee. I scored 97 percent, and he scored 83 percent. Of course, you have got to remember, this was 'Mad Dog' Lewis doing the grading. Plus, the coaches used me to motivate Woerner. They played games with his head."

"Scott was kind of a free-spirited guy," secondary coach Bill Lewis agreed. "Scott had great respect for that program and never would do anything that would hurt that team. There were times that he needed to be encouraged to practice with the intensity that we needed.

"But what a playmaker! You can talk about that worn-out expression, 'big players making big plays in big games,' but that was Scott.

"Still, Scott would not start unless he had practiced the way we wanted him to practice. Sometimes it was right up to kickoff until we decided and felt that Scott had earned the right to start the game. He went out there and played lights out. But he needed to have that hanging over him.

"What also happens with a player like Scott," Bill continued, "is the expectation level is so high. He was one of the special players on that team based on previous performance. Sometimes we as coaches get carried away with that."

Woerner himself said two knee surgeries had slowed him down by 1980.

"Bill Lewis saved my career," he said. "The name of the game was 'don't get beat deep.' What I could do in 1978, I couldn't do in 1980. I had had two knee surgeries, and I was bigger. I was stronger, but

I was not as fast. It was more brains than speed. Bill Lewis was the first real secondary coach I had. I learned so much about the game from him."

THE DEFINITION OF A MAN

As far as Chris Welton is concerned, Scott Woerner epitomizes the definition of "a man's man."

Welton and Woerner were close at Georgia, and two decades later they still talk to each other often.

"He is the salt of the earth," Welton said of his pal.

Welton considered himself a technically proficient football player. His teammates were always jealous of his seemingly photographic memory. He displayed that intelligence in the way he played the game.

By contrast, Woerner played a more swashbuckling brand of football.

"Scott was just a gambler on the football field," Welton said. "If you were playing football, and the stakes weren't so high, and it was really just a game, you'd like to think you played the game like Scott.

"But I was always just trying to make sure I was doing the right thing. Rather than making a big play, I was trying not to get beat. Scott was the other way around."

One of the changes that secondary coach Bill Lewis brought to the team in 1980 was a more disciplined approach to the art and skill of playing the secondary.

"Bill Lewis is a perfectionist," Welton said. "His attention to detail is incredible. We went from a system of, 'Hell, just line up and knock the shit out of them!' which was Jim Pyburn's methodology, to Lewis, who if you are supposed to be lined up three yards outside the hash mark and you are two and a half yards outside, you got a minus. If you were supposed to take the first step with your right foot and you took it with your left, you got a minus. As a result, I don't think Scott graded out with a winning grade. Scott was just going to do his thing. He was a gambler, and it drove Lewis crazy. His MO was to get beat deep in the first half and then in the second half come up with great plays.

"But ask anybody who was the best defensive back, and it was Scott."

Woerner had played his high school football at Jonesboro High south of Atlanta, where he quarterbacked for Weyman Sellers, who had coached Fran Tarkenton, Paul Gilbert, and Andy Johnson at

Scott Woerner returned a punt 67 yards for a touchdown and
returned an interception 98 yards against Clemson.

Athens High. They had all gone on to become starting quarterbacks at Georgia.

But originally Woerner was going to Texas.

"I was born and raised there until I was 10 or 11 years old," Woerner explained. "But when I went out there to visit, Darrell Royal announced in the locker room that he was resigning that night.

"I look back at it now and see the integrity of the man."

WOERNER ROLLS SIX

Although Scott Woerner did not start the Clemson game, it did not take him long to stamp his imprint on the game.

Clemson received the kickoff but failed to make a first down. Woerner returned the punt 67 yards for a touchdown.

He and Jake Scott were probably the two best punt returners we ever had. Buzy Rosenberg was awfully good, as was Wayne Swinford. Scott might have had a little more speed than Woerner, but not much. He could motor, too. He was stronger than the others. You couldn't arm-tackle him.

"We used a form of what we called a middle return," Bill Lewis explained. "We never changed it all year. We would bring three guys back in front of Scott [Woerner], usually the secondary guys on the field. They formed a semi-wedge eight to 10 yards in front of Scott. We tried to get the middle guy to block the first or most dangerous guy. Our goal was to make one first down, to get a 10-yard return.

"We spent a lot of time on it in practice. After practice I would keep the punters and we would get in a bunch of reps without having to keep the whole team."

Incredibly, Woerner got himself in the doghouse on the touchdown when he knelt down in the end zone and flung the football out like he was rolling dice. I had to chastise him for that.

The punt return was a fortuitous start for us, but it was not immediately apparent what kind of game it was going to be. But in the first half our offense ran 11 offensive plays and failed to make a first down. Still, we were ahead at halftime 14-10.

"In an average game, you play about 63 to 65 plays," Frank Ros explained. "Clemson had the ball like 98 plays that day."

The actual numbers from the play-by-play chart show that in the first half, Clemson controlled the ball 60 plays to our 11 plays. We did better in the second half, but Clemson ran 95 plays to our 49.

Woerner rolls six in the end zone after returning a punt for a touch-down. I chastised him for this display of showmanship.

"We were dying," Greg Bell recalled. "We were all rotating in. Everybody played a lot that day, because it was hot and the offense absolutely sucked."

"We couldn't do anything," offensive guard Tim Morrison agreed. "I don't know if it was play-calling or inability to hit the guys hard enough. We were fortunate to have great individual players. Scott Woerner was a phenomenal athlete."

After Woerner's touchdown, Clemson drove from its 20 to our 30 in 14 plays before they missed a 47-yard field goal. So it was not until halfway through the first quarter that our offense even got on the field. We went three and out.

Clemson came right back down the field, and this time they got all the way to our 11 before Woerner intercepted a pass in our end zone. He ran it back 98 yards to their two-yard line. Two plays later, our quarterback, Buck Belue, sneaked in, and we were ahead 14-0 after five offensive plays and no first downs.

A NOD TO DANNY FORD

For Scott Woerner, the best part of the interception return was that it was on the sideline in front of the Clemson bench. He can still picture the face of Clemson coach Danny Ford. It would have been sweeter if he had been able to score, but he ran out of gas, plus he was being chased by Chuck McSwain, a fast tailback.

"I always kidded him that it was the offensive guard who caught him inside the five," Bill Lewis said.

Greg Bell maintains Woerner broke technique on his 98-yard interception return. Indeed, it was for that reason that he was able to make the play.

"We had a man-to-man near the goal line," Bell recalled. "Woerner was on the left side, and there was no wide receiver. So he was five yards off the tight end like he was supposed to be.

"Clemson put Perry Tuttle out on the wide receiver, and the safety, Jeff Hipp, came out on him. Tuttle came out and put one of the first spin moves on him. Meanwhile, Woerner was watching the quarterback.

"You never leave your wing man. I would have been on that tight end like a duck on a June bug. But Woerner was just floating across the field like, 'I'm out on a skate,' and as he floats across, the quarterback throws it, and he picks it off.

"That's the difference," Bell continued. "That's the game breaker that he was."

"The rest of us were lined up where we were supposed to be, but that in and of itself was a great combination," Welton said. "Everybody had to be doing what they were supposed to be doing generally, but you have to have somebody make a great play, and that was Scott."

CLEMSON RALLIES

At halftime in the locker room, it looked like the offense was a bunch of tourists and the defense had been in a war zone. The offense didn't even have a first down, but we still led 14-10.

The offense finally got a little something going in the third quarter. Our first two drives led to field goals. Herschel Walker gained most of the yards. The second drive was set up by an interception by our defensive end, Robert Miles.

"I don't remember the specifics of the play," Miles said. "I remember it was something where I was on the back side of most of the action. The quarterback threw it back, and he was not expecting me to be dropping off. I was out there with no one to cover, in no man's land, and he put one out there he shouldn't have.

"I ended up going all the way to the other side with my little return. I was running east and west. I gained maybe five yards."

Danny Ford was going back and forth with his quarterbacks between Mike Gasque and Homer Jordan. Jordan went to Cedar Shoals in Athens. I believe he had followed Anthony Arnold as their quarterback. He used to sell drinks in the stands at our home games. We recruited Jordan. I don't remember why he didn't come to Georgia, but obviously we did not do a very good job of recruiting him.

Clemson was able to get a couple more field goals, but we gave them one more chance when our punter Jim Broadway dropped a snap. That gave them the ball at our 41.

"Mike Garrett and Bucky Dilts, the punters before always told me, 'You will drop one somewhere, sometime in your career,'" punter Jim Broadway recalled.

"The ball was on the 40, so all I had to do was pop it up. It was a low snap and hit the ground and went back between my legs. I just laid on it. Then they drove it back down the field."

A HIPP-POCKET WIN

The game centered on Scott Woerner one more time, when he was called for pass interference, setting up Clemson with a first-and-goal just inside the Georgia 10. This time safety Jeff Hipp saved the win for us.

Hipp grew up a Clemson fan, even in West Columbia, South Carolina.

"My father graduated from Clemson," he said. "I grew up a Tiger fan. Back then, Clemson was having some struggles. My senior year in high school, Georgia came into the picture. They were a top-10 program then, and that catches a kid's eye. I had a nice official visit, and I fell in love with the campus and with the players here at the time. It was a total contrast to what I saw at Clemson.

"Another reason I came to Georgia was that they told me I could play quarterback. Clemson told me upfront I would be moved to defensive back. And I wanted to play baseball, too. I lettered one year as a pitcher at Georgia. But after having knee surgery and fighting for a position trying to do both, I gave up baseball to concentrate on football."

Hipp had intercepted two passes in the 42-0 rout of Texas A&M. With Clemson threatening with just a little more than two minutes to play, he intercepted his third pass of the season.

"It was a little post pattern, and the ball ricocheted off Frank Ros's headgear," Hipp said. "It went straight up. There was a fight for the ball, and I was able to leap up and grab it. I thought I was in the end zone and fell back near the one."

Hipp had average speed, but he had great timing, a great feel, and great anticipation for the football.

Clemson had done a pretty good job up to that point of holding Herschel Walker in check, but he brought it out of our end zone on a key third down. It was third and four from our seven, and he took it 20 yards, and we could finally run out the clock.

"We didn't play well, but good teams are going to play some bad games," Welton said. "Good teams that find a way to win wind up being great teams. We managed to find a way. Nobody was discouraged, and that was early enough that we didn't feel like we had dodged a bullet."

The statistics may have favored Clemson, but the 20-16 score favored Georgia.

When you look at the statistical comparison at the end of the season, it reflects what happened in these games. I think we were outgained, and they had the ball more in the year-end stats. You could not look at those stats and tell that this team won the game.

WHERE IS MY CAR?

Defensive lineman Tim Crowe knows that Scott Woerner had a great game against Clemson, because he has been told so, and because he has watched films of the game. But even though he played in the game, he has no personal recollections of the game.

"I got a concussion," Crowe explained. "I see it on film, but I don't remember Scott having a career game. Frank Ros had to call timeout to get me off the field. I was standing in the Clemson huddle.

"I came to my senses probably the next day. I didn't know where my car was parked. I can remember everything that happened the rest of my career, but nothing comes from that game."

Chapter Eight

TCU TO UK

A BIG EFFORT

We played four games between the Clemson game and the South Carolina game. The teams we played—TCU, Mississippi, Vanderbilt, and Kentucky—were teams that on paper we were expected to beat. But we approached each one of them seriously. Our team was gaining confidence, but the seniors on that team did not want to endure another season like 1979.

Look at any championship team, and for the most part they are able either to avoid injuries or overcome them when they happen.

That was the case in 1980. We had few injuries that kept our key players out of action for long, and when we did, we always had someone step to the forefront.

A case in point is our win over TCU. Herschel Walker injured his ankle in that game, and as a result, he didn't play any after the first quarter. But his roommate, Barry Young, responded and gained 83 yards for us and scored a touchdown in helping us win.

Young was a good tailback. He was from Swainsboro, which was just down the road from Walker's hometown of Wrightsville. Mike Cavan recruited them both, and they roomed together for three years.

"He didn't have Herschel's speed," Mike said. "He had tremendous vision and moves, but he didn't have the great speed."

It was a tight game until Walker made a super 41-yard run to set up our first touchdown. Unfortunately, on that play, when he was tackled, the defender's facemask caught his ankle at just the wrong angle. So after that Young carried the load. Melvin Simmons came in late in the game and carried the ball, too.

Simmons lettered for us for four years, but he was always in Walker's shadow. But we used him all over the field. We put him at wide receiver and threw hitches to him. He was on special teams. He did a lot of things.

It seemed like every spring that he was the leading rusher in the G-Day game. He went on to a fine career in the Navy.

We scored right at the end of the half again in this game. Buck Belue made a couple of nice runs, and then he threw a 28-yard touchdown pass to Chuck Jones with just 12 seconds to go in the half.

We had great field position that time, getting the ball on our own 47 with 35 seconds to go, a wonderful scoring opportunity that we capitalized on.

HIJINKS IN THE SECONDARY

Scott Woerner intercepted a pass for us in the second half, but some of the old option quarterback must have come out in him, because he immediately lateraled the ball to our safety, Jeff Hipp.

Hipp had jammed his foot late in the Clemson game, so he had been sort of limping around most of the TCU game.

"Scott was able to intercept the ball," Hipp said, "but as soon as he did, the receiver wrapped his arms around him. But he spun around and tossed the ball back to me. I ran another 30 yards down the field."

Freddie Gilbert, a fine freshman defensive end on that team, intercepted a pass at the line of scrimmage and ran it back down to the TCU 11-yard line, and that set up Barry Young's touchdown.

Gilbert was the first player we had signed out of Griffin, Georgia, in a few years, and we had to work like heck to get him. We found out when he got here that he couldn't see, but once we got his vision corrected, he became a great player for us. He had such a great wingspan that it was hard to get around him and hard to pass over him. He and Jimmy Payne became the greatest tackle duo we had had at Georgia since George Patton and Bill Stanfill in the late 1960s.

THE FILM WAS LOST(?)

TCU was down that year, winning just one game. F.A. Dry was their head coach. His son was a linebacker on the team. They had a freshman wide receiver named Stanley Washington, and he was an All-American the next year.

But even without Herschel Walker for three quarters, we won decisively, 34-3. We recovered three fumbles and intercepted two passes, and we had seven sacks and five more tackles behind the line. They finished with −10 yards rushing.

Pat McShea had a particularly good game that day, but he remembers that we didn't even show the players film of TCU before the game.

"They were so pitiful that we didn't even watch film," McShea said. "The staff acted like the film was lost or destroyed."

That made him nervous, because he was one of those players who liked to study the film and know who he was up against. It didn't seem to bother him too much. He had three blocked passes, a couple of sacks, caused a fumble, and recovered a fumble.

Of course, when he wasn't in, there was when Freddie Gilbert intercepted that pass and nearly ran it in for a touchdown.

"MEAT CLEAVER"

One of the reasons our run defense was so strong that year was because of Eddie Weaver.

"Defenses win championships," cornerback Scott Woerner said, repeating a cliché. "If they don't score, you can't lose. For us it all began around Eddie Weaver up front. It took two guys to handle him."

Weaver was practically a mythical figure, even among his teammates. He was large, and he lived large.

Dan Magill, our sports publicist for many years, gave Weaver the nickname "Meat Cleaver." That really caught on. Everyone absolutely loved it.

Jim Blakewood, who blocked Weaver every day in practice, said, "He was the hardest person to block I ever blocked anywhere, anytime. He was quick as a cat and used his hands well. He could bullrush you. His center of gravity was low. Even the junior and senior linemen when we were freshmen were having trouble with him."

It was common for players to barge in on each other at the dorm whenever they ordered pizzas. Some of them made a habit of looking for the delivery guy and following him to the room.

"Eddie would order two large pizzas and lock himself in," Pat McShea laughed.

"Go away!" Weaver would shout as he closed the door.

At about six foot one, Weaver was not particularly tall, and he carried a good bit of weight for that time.

"Eddie was a guy who really wanted to prove that he could weigh 290 or whatever he wanted to weigh and still do the things that he was supposed to do," Erk Russell said. "It became pretty obvious he was not conditioning himself."

That usually meant extra running, which meant supervision for Erk.

"There is no telling how many hours I spent after practice, watching him plod around and pant and drop to a knee," Erk complained.

Erk got the idea to take Weaver over to a water tank in the physical education department where they submerge you and check your body fat.

"We had an off day during spring practice, so I took all the defensive linemen over there," Erk recalled. "They have simpler ways of doing it now, but we had to use a snorkel and get down in the water and stay there a minute or so."

The numbers surprised Erk. Weaver's body fat was not as bad as that of some of his teammates.

"But I bloated it," Erk confessed. "I toned some of the others down, and I raised his up where the number meant he was obese."

He responded to Erk's chiding and began to work harder at conditioning.

"He took so much pride in his strength," Erk said. "He was strong."

"We used to call him 'Thursday Eddie,'" fellow down lineman Tim Crowe recalled. "About Thursday he was ready to go full speed. He would knock the hell out of you when we didn't have anything on but helmets and shoulder pads."

He was responsible for one of the few times that Erk lost his temper. For some reason, he used to pound on the scout-team quarterback Jeff Paulk.

"The coaches would tell us to go 75 percent or 50 percent, but Eddie would fly through the air and slam on Paulk," linebacker Frank Ros said.

Such an incident pushed Erk over the edge one day.

"Get out of here!" he shouted. "We don't put up with this."

Weaver was from Haines City, Florida, and he and Joe Creamons, who was from Eustis, Florida, developed a pretty close relationship.

"I used to take him home," Creamons said. "I used to drop him off at a Holiday Inn on the highway, and his parents would pick him up.

"Eddie is a very intelligent individual," Creamons said.

Both played guard, but not the same position.

"Thank goodness," Creamons confessed.

Weaver's brother, Mike, came to Georgia and was a starting offensive guard for us and was a really good player. When I went down to Haines City to recruit Mike, Weaver was there with the family, but he stayed in the background.

"This is Mike's time, not mine," he said.

He got himself out of the way and didn't want to be in the middle of it, because he didn't want to distract from Mike. It was such a touching thing.

They came from a solid family. They were all smart. Mike got his degree and has been in banking. They had another brother who is a doctor.

"Eddie was proud of his athletic prowess," defensive end Robert Miles responded. "You didn't have to say a lot to him. You didn't need to get in his face. All you had to do was say, 'Weave, you're on me.' He knew he was getting blown out."

Invariably, he responded, "I'm from Haines City, Florida, and I'm one of the best athletes! I won the state shot! I can run a 4.5!"

THE STEELE MAN

There was another player who didn't know the meaning of half speed, and that was Mike Steele. Mike was the most incredible player we ever had. I have never known a more relentless football player or one who had more energy than Mike Steele. He stayed on the football team for five years as a walk-on. He never received financial aid and never missed one day of practice in five years.

We even named an award after him, the Steele Man Award. He was the first and only winner.

To win it, you had to go through every practice without missing a day. He not only did that, he went through five spring practices. We never had anybody who came back for a spring practice after his senior season.

He was a walk-on from nearby Statham, Georgia. During two-a-day sessions, Steele would drive back home, about 15 miles away, and work on the farm with his father, come back to afternoon practice, and then go back and work more chores with his dad.

That is absolutely incredible during two-a-days, because most players struggled to get from the practice field to the dormitory and back to the practice field for the next session.

"No matter what day it was, Mike was going to give you 100 percent," Tim Crowe said. "Coach Russell would say three-quarters speed, which meant basically you walked. But Mike would keep going full speed."

Three stars and a sub—quarterback Buck Belue (8), defensive tackle Jimmy Payne (87), career substitute Mike Steele (70), and tailback Herschel Walker (34)—made amazing contributions to the Bulldog squad.

"I got to get better," Steele would say.

"Weaver used to try to kill him," Crowe said. "He would forearm him, and there would be blood all over his face."

The blood came from a screw in his facemask that could have been cut off, but he never did.

"Blood makes me tough," he said.

Steele did not actually play in a game in 1980. He really only played in the 44-0 win over Tennessee in the 1981 season opener.

He always wanted to be in special forces. When he was in the ROTC, he used to rappel. We got a call one night from the campus police that they had arrested Steele because they caught him rappelling off the bridge by the stadium. He was just innocently doing that.

His greatest claim to fame came in Somalia when he was a chalk leader in the *Black Hawk Down* incident. He was dropped by helicopter into the heart of Mogadishu, Somalia, to abduct two lieutenants of a Samalian warlord. The action was supposed to take just an hour, but it turned into a long and terrible night of fighting thousands of armed Somalians. It was the longest sustained firefight involving American soldiers since the Vietnam War.

He was decorated with the Bronze Star with valor for his role in the battle. Because he lost some of his men in the battle, he does not like to talk about it.

He had a staph infection in a leg later and nearly died. They read last rites. He was in real bad shape.

The television in Steele's hospital room was showing *The Flintstones*.

"Here I am fixing to kick the bucket, and I'm watching *The Flintstones*," Steele mused. An iron-man competition would have been more appropriate.

"He got out of bed and walked down the hall and got on a treadmill and passed all those blood clots through his lungs," Crowe said. "If there was ever going to be a hero, he is my hero."

Crowe's hero today wears support pantyhose because of the wounds to his legs as protection against further blood clots.

I can say without hesitation that if I had to make a choice to be in a foxhole with my life on the line in military combat, there is no one I would choose over Mike Steele.

FIND THE BALL!

Jim Broadway gave way to Mark Malkiewicz as our punter from the TCU game on. He continued to hold on placements, but his kicking gave us one more memory that year.

We were having punt practice one day, and Broadway was punting. John Kasay always liked to emphasize to the team that they needed to know where the ball was, so he would yell, "Find the ball! Find the ball!" He probably said that a thousand times.

Well, one day it was windy and the ball hung up. As usual, John was shouting, "Find the ball!" and it came down and hit him right on top of the head. Everybody was looking around to see how to react, so when I laughed, everybody else broke up with laughter.

Broadway ran from one end of the field to continue the drill and Wayne McDuffie told him, "You are damn lucky Coach Dooley is out here, because otherwise Kasay would kill you."

John didn't say anything, but the next day he comes out to practice wearing his helmet from his playing days and a t-shirt he had printed up that said, "Find the ball!"

"The worst thing I could have done was get angry over that," John said.

It Never Seems Easy

Mike Cavan said Herschel Walker could have gained 300 yards on Mississippi that year, but Walker was still not full strength from the ankle he sprained against TCU. I really think that was the first injury that Walker had ever had, and he was a little timid about coming back.

As it turned out, he had 48 yards on just 10 carries in the game, but he got some key yards late in the game when Mississippi was trying to rally on us. But sophomore Carnie Norris picked up 150 yards for us on 15 carries in that game.

"That was the only time I played a whole game," Norris explained. "It was an opportune time for me. I was in the right place at the right time."

Norris was an elusive running back, but he just did not have the speed to be a breakaway runner. But he accepted his role as a backup. It seems he always had a good game against Mississippi, too.

We played Ole Miss every year, but it was not a game that our fans got too excited about. For one thing, whenever we went to Oxford, it is a hard place to travel to. And for another, Ole Miss was usually not highly ranked when we played them. But they still beat us plenty of times.

The great teams we had in 1975 and 1976 lost in Oxford in back-to-back years. Both times we just dominated the first quarter and looked like we were going to rout them, but we let down, and they came back and beat us. That was the only game that 1976 team lost during the regular season.

In 1980, they came in with a 1-4 record, but their quarterback, big John Fourcade, was leading the conference in total offense, averaging 225 yards a game. We held him in check somewhat. He passed for 162 yards and a touchdown, but we intercepted him three times, too. But we were our own worst enemy.

For example, Scott Woerner returned a punt 45 yards into Ole Miss territory, but we fumbled it. Then he returned another one 38 yards to their 18, and we had to settle for a field goal after a penalty. Then Bob Kelly intercepted Fourcade to put us on their end of the field again, and we had to try a 51-yard field goal, and Rex Robinson missed.

We finally took advantage of field position the next play when Eddie Weaver recovered a fumble. Buck Belue threw to Anthony Arnold for a 34-yard touchdown.

The last three minutes of the half were wild. Norris gave us a shot with a 41-yard run, and we were able to push it in when Norris scored on a short run with just 44 seconds to go in the half. So for the third time that year, we scored near the end of the half.

The funny thing is we had a chance to score again. Our safety, Jeff Hipp, intercepted Fourcade with 18 seconds to go in the half. But on the next play, Belue threw an interception, and they ran it in from 32 yards out with just nine seconds to go in the half.

It was a screen pass, and Belue just didn't get it high enough. He kind of lobbed it.

The third quarter was the kind of quarter that would drive me nuts. We missed a field goal. Then Ole Miss scored. We intercepted a pass only to fumble it.

We finally made a field goal early in the fourth quarter, and then Norris and Walker combined to help us drive for another touchdown. We went for two, and Belue threw it to Charles Junior. There were only six minutes to go, but we had a two-touchdown lead.

But not for long. Fourcade brought them back again. We almost intercepted him twice, and we had a sack nullified by a penalty, and they scored with less than two minutes to go. Of course, they went for an onside kick, but we got it, and one of our fullbacks, Ronnie Stewart, made a 13-yard run to help us kill the clock in a 28-21 game that should not have been that close.

BLINDSIDED

Before the Vanderbilt game I was in a car wreck.

Barbara had gotten involved chairing a spirit committee at the university. Part of that committee's role was to paint the town. We wanted to go downtown to see what kind of job the fraternities and sororities had done.

Derek, our youngest child, was playing for a city league team on Thursday nights. So we picked Derek up, and we were driving downtown, when all of a sudden—wham!

We were hit by somebody who we found out later had run three red lights. The police were chasing him. He hit us on the rear driver's side, which is about where Derek was. Thank goodness he still had his football uniform on.

I was not my usual active self on the sideline at the Vanderbilt game because I had been in a car wreck a couple of days earlier.

My face went right down and blasted my mouth. I was bleeding everywhere and was in a daze.

Barbara looked like nothing was wrong with her. She was knocked up against the front of car. They released me, but the doctors wanted to keep her overnight. Sometimes the spleen will take a while before it fills up and breaks. I was woozy and punchy, but I talked them into sending me home.

Sure enough, the next morning, Barbara's spleen burst, and they had to remove it. Meanwhile, I went and met the team. My upper lip was down to my chin, and I told them, "I got the hell knocked out of me! I have not been hit that hard since a Mississippi State defensive end hit me when I was running the option at Auburn. But I'm ready to go now."

The doctors gave me a little something, because I had a bad concussion. I was woozy on the sidelines. Dick Copas was our get-back coach. His job was always to keep people back, because if you get too far out, you get a penalty. We were always an enthusiastic sideline team.

Dick was following me around that day, because I was leaning and looking like I was going to fall. I probably did on occasion.

I had a habit of reacting after a play that I was not even aware of at first. In fact, I used to be sore after games and didn't know why. But if you watch films of me on the sideline, during the play I might kick or run a few yards. I nailed a few assistant coaches over the years.

WALKER GETS WELL AGAINST VANDERBILT

Vanderbilt was consistently as bad as anybody in the league. But just as consistently, they took us to the wire. They beat us up there one time and tied us one time, which was the worst tie I can remember. It was in 1984, a game I remember because I was mad at everybody, starting with myself. I did a poor job, but it seemed like everybody—the managers, the trainers, the players, the coaches, and even the team doctors—was up there having a party.

In 1980, they came in without a win. Herschel Walker had 202 yards by halftime. He could have had 400 if I had left him in the game. I never did try to break records just to break records. Plus, there was the possibility of him getting hurt.

We just dominated them from early on. I remember on Walker's last touchdown run, a 53-yarder, that he just kind of coasted. He never really got into a speed stride. He'd already had a 60-yard run and a 48-yard run, and I think they were kind of avoiding him. We beat them 41-0.

GIVE US A BREAK

Herschel Walker's breakaway ability meant that our defense spent a lot more time on the field even though we were moving and scoring the ball.

"I remember our defense used to get so frustrated," Tim Crowe said. "You don't want your defense on the field the whole time, because that means the offense is not doing its job. But we were on the field the whole time because Herschel would score from 60 yards out in two plays, and we would be right back in the game."

When Carnie Norris came in to relieve Walker, the defenders knew they might get a breather. But with Walker's breakaway ability, they might be back in the game at any time.

THE DORM LIFE

Every Thursday night a group of players got together in the dorm for a little low-stakes poker game. As long as the team kept winning, it became a ritual. The regulars included Marty Ballard, Bob Kelly, Frank Ros, Mike Fisher, Chris Welton, Hugh Nall, and Pat McShea. Some others drifted in and out.

"We played a game called three-four," Ballard said. "I couldn't even tell you how to play anymore. It seems like Hugh did most of the winning."

Ballard, on the other hand, was a habitual loser for the first five or six weeks.

"After that, we got superstitious that Marty had to lose," Fisher said. "He quit playing, and we just put his money in and made sure he lost."

We called Ballard a player-coach that year. He was big and had a great attitude, but he never developed into a good football player. So he watched the tackles during the game and helped Wayne McDuffie. Ballard is another one who has stayed connected to the team through the years. He had a brief fling with stardom when a television series based on the movie *Breaking Away* was filmed in Athens. Ballard was cast as a football player in the series. Neither Ballard nor the series lasted long.

MOTHER KASAY

John Kasay and his family lived at the dorm. He was well suited for that assignment.

"I was not put in the dorm because I was going to run it like a penitentiary," John said. "I was put there to run it right."

He maintained order, no small feat with that many competitive young men, and he took care of some things on his own.

"I used to ask the players," he said, "do you want me to take care of it, or do you want me to take you over there and throw you in front of Coach Dooley's desk?"

He supervised the annual rat court, which was an initiation for freshmen. A veteran player would be voted "grand dragon" by his teammates. It was a testament to the camaraderie of the team that one of the grand dragons in 1980 was Nat Hudson, a black athlete.

Most of the stuff that went on at the dorm could be described as mischief.

"We were always playing jokes on each other," recalled Pat McShea, a defensive end.

Once after a fishing trip, McShea took a bream and taped it under a desk in Jay Russell's room. They noticed the smell the second day, and by the third day, they were frantic to find it. When Russell finally located the fish on the fourth day, he put it in a bucket of water rigged to splash on McShea's carpet when a door was opened.

Keith Middleton was the butt of a McShea joke, too, after coming back from a rattlesnake roundup in Washington, Georgia, a community about 25 miles east of Athens. Middleton was drunk and passed out on his bed. McShea and his teammates taped him to the mattress and put the mattress on the balcony, which led to a crazed reaction when Middleton woke up.

John headed off a disaster in 1980 when he discovered the whole starting secondary out too late before the season opener.

"It was right after two-a-days," John recalled. "You have to remember, these are young men. They had been in camp for two solid weeks, and that does get overbearing. Right after two-a-days ended was their first opportunity to get out."

On his normal rounds, he noticed the absence of Scott Woerner, Jeff Hipp, Mike Fisher, and Chris Welton.

"A pattern started to develop," he said, "and I was getting angry, because 1979 had not been a very good year. I wanted to get off to a good start."

When Woerner made it to bed that night, he was shocked to find John waiting for him in his bed.

"I told them I wasn't going to say anything, but they better win, because if they didn't, they were going to be drug up to the office," John said.

"Of course we won, and I was happy after the game, but they came out of that locker room grinning like a jackass in a briar patch. They dodged a bullet."

But John's sense of justice required some retribution, which was settled in the coming days with extra conditioning work.

Pat McShea always felt like he put one over on John.

"I took a night class one quarter, so it was always late when I got back to the dorm, but it was legit," McShea said.

"Late class?" John would ask as McShea exited his car with books.

"From then on, I always had night class," McShea winked. "I would just keep books in my car."

In retrospect, I'm kind of glad that I didn't know *everything* that went on.

THE KENTUCKY GAME

After the Vanderbilt game, we had to go on the road for just the second time that season, to Kentucky.

We decided to wear the silver pants instead of the red. We felt like we had something going, and the "silver britches" were part of it.

Kentucky was always a hard-hitting team, and that was the way we presented them to the players. Part of that was the fact that John Kasay was the designated scout for them, and he probably remembered back to the time when he played.

They always had some tough guys, but either they didn't have any reserve strength or they were in terrible condition, because usually we could pull away late. We used to call it a barroom brawl.

John calculated that from 1980 to 1983, when Georgia was 43-3-1 that 17 of those wins came in the last four minutes.

"We would watch the other team wilt," he said. "We would just take the game away from them. The game no longer meant anything to them. They were spent."

Such histrionics were not necessary for us in 1980, a 27-0 win. In 1978, we had to make a dramatic comeback. We scored 10 points in the fourth quarter, and Rex Robinson kicked a 29-yard field goal with three seconds to play to win 17-16.

"Yeah! Yeah! Yeah!" shouted Larry Munson on the radio.

I remember when we lined up for that kick that one of our tackles didn't run on the field for the kick. That meant our end would be short, and they would block the kick. I looked up, and the tackle was standing next to me.

"What are you doing here?" I asked him as I put my arms around him.

"Praying, Coach."

"Well, your prayers just got answered, because Kentucky has called a timeout, which enables me to get your broad rear into the game."

THE 91-YARD PASS PLAY NO ONE SAW

Buck Belue threw to Anthony Arnold for a 91-yard touchdown. It was just a simple out and up. Kentucky was crowding us.

It was the second longest pass play in Georgia history up to that point, but not many Georgia fans saw it. And of course, it didn't have near the impact that the Belue-to-Lindsay Scott play would in a couple of weeks.

Arnold seemed to be cast in Scott's shadow by the press, but he made some great plays for us. Of course, everybody remembers the 1978 Georgia Tech game when he caught a 42-yard pass from Belue in the fourth quarter and then scored the two-point conversion on an option pitch in a game we won 29-28.

"It was not anything special, other than I had a chance to touch the ball," Arnold said. "If I look back over my career, I think I could have done a whole lot more if I had had more opportunities."

Receivers coach Charlie Whittemore called him the "quickest receiver I ever had." That was never more evident than at Kentucky.

"When he caught that ball, there was a defensive back and three linebackers close enough to reach out and touch him," Charlie recalled. "None of them did. We had this little pass that was simply throw it to Amp and see what he could do with it. You see a lot of teams now run what they call a tunnel screen. That was a tunnel screen without the tunnel."

Arnold had been a splendid high school quarterback at Cedar Shoals in Athens, and he was even recruited by Louisville to play basketball.

Charlie felt that he could have been a successful professional player had he not been injured after a brief stint with the Denver Broncos.

"He could make things happen," Charlie recalled. "He would have been a lot like Hines Ward, very much like him. Maybe not as thick as Hines, but he was that kind of player."

A CRACK IN THE ARMOR

One of our key seniors, center Hugh Nall, had been injured before the Kentucky game. In fact, we did not expect him to come back for the rest of the year.

Wayne McDuffie, the tough guy, wrote a letter to Nall expressing his appreciation for how hard Nall had worked and how hard he had played. It was another side of Wayne that the players seldom saw.

Nall kept a copy of the letter, but he sent the original to Wayne's widow, Toni, after his death.

Nall had been voted captain for the Kentucky game, but when he got hurt, he didn't expect to make the trip. In fact, he had already contacted some friends about getting a ride home for the weekend. But Wednesday night, I told him that we wanted him to make the trip.

When the officials called for the captains to go out for the coin toss, Nall was not going to go onto the field.

"Everybody turned and waited on me," he said. "They made me go out and call the coin toss, and after the game they gave me the game ball. That was the kind of team we played for."

Chapter Nine

SOUTH CAROLINA

THE HISTORY

T he first time I coached against South Carolina was in my first year, 1964, and we tied 7-7. Dan Reeves was their quarterback. But we didn't lose another game to South Carolina until 1978.

So although I had had good success against South Carolina, a lot of the players on the 1980 team had never beaten them. We won up there in 1977, and that was my 100th career victory. Steve Rogers, a transfer from Navy, came off the bench to quarterback us that night. We had five fumbles in that game, which was a problem all year. In fact, we led the country in fumbles that year.

That was one reason we abandoned the Veer Offense and switched to the I Formation in 1978, and we were fortunate that Willie McClendon developed into an outstanding tailback. But the one game we lost during the 1978 season was at South Carolina. McClendon had a long run, but that was about all we did. It was also the first time that we wore red pants.

So after playing in Columbia, South Carolina, back-to-back years, we played then in Athens in 1979 and 1980. They beat us in 1979. In fact, that was our third straight loss to start the season. That was the only time that ever happened to one of my teams.

ON THE NATIONAL STAGE

Obviously, circumstances were drastically different in 1980 as the game approached. We were 7-0 and ranked fourth, the highest we had been since late in the 1976 season. South Carolina was coming in 6-1, including a win over Michigan and climbing in the polls. They had lost a close game to Southern Cal.

The game was going to be nationally televised, which was unusual then. There were rules then that restricted the number of times you could be on television, so this was going to be the first opportunity the nation had to see Herschel Walker in action.

Of course, South Carolina had its own outstanding tailback in George Rogers, who was from Duluth. He was one of those who got away.

As I recall, the coach at his high school had some influence. He might have steered Rogers toward South Carolina, thinking that was a better situation for him. I know the coach was not too friendly to us.

By the time they came to Athens in 1980, Rogers already had more than 1,000 yards rushing and was averaging 6.4 yards a carry. Walker's numbers were very similar: 877 yards and an average of 6.2 per carry. Rogers had 10 touchdowns and Walker had nine. And they each seemed to break at least one long run every game.

It was one of those showdowns that got the press and the fans excited. Rogers was a senior, so he had been considered a Heisman Trophy candidate all year. But Walker as a freshman had surprised the nation, and he was just beginning to get some mention. It was unheard of then to think that a freshman could be a candidate for such an award.

We had a routine for home games, of course, including a devotion and the pregame meal. I would make some remarks to the team, and then each of the coordinators would say something. Erk Russell kind of summed up what this particular game was all about.

"Men, look outside. The sun is shining. The birds are singing. It's a beautiful day. We're on national TV. We're No. 4. They're No. 14. They've got George. We've got Herschel. God Almighty! What an opportunity!"

"If anybody else in the world says that, you think, 'Man, that's stupid.' But with Coach Russell," Chris Welton said, "man, we were ready to play!"

ANOTHER FAMOUS PLAY

The play that stands out in the South Carolina game is the long run that Herschel Walker made. That play, next to the Buck Belue-to-Lindsay Scott play, is probably the most replayed play in Georgia football history. That is when the whole country got a glimpse of Walker, when they saw his speed. They really couldn't believe it. There were three separate people with angles, and they couldn't get him.

Erk Russell always knew how to talk to his players to get them fired up for a game.

It was a simple draw play. The quarterback brings the ball back to him. He delays, and the line direction blocks, that is they take the defender where he wants to go. Walker was to read the blocks. It plays into the hands of a defense that is rushing up the field in a hurry. With Walker back there, it was probably as good a play as we had.

It turned out to be a big play, as it was the only touchdown we scored. We had first and 10 on their 11-yard line in the first quarter and missed a short field goal. And then near the end of the half, we had first and goal on their four-yard line. We called a timeout on fourth and one, and I don't remember the specifics, but I just remember that we screwed up a fake. It was a fake run and then throwing the ball with no option to run. I remember that I didn't like the call, but it was already done.

So we were ahead 3-0 at the half, and it could have easily have been 17-0. They might have had a little momentum at halftime because they had stopped us on the goal line, but Walker took away that momentum right away.

It was the third play of the third quarter, third and six at our 24. He started up the middle and cut to the right sideline and outran everybody 76 yards. There were a lot of backs who could have made a first down, and a few who could have made 20 or 30 yards, but there were not very many who could have gone all of the way on that play.

"I had never seen anybody do that before," fullback Jimmy Womack agreed. "Herschel was headed at the sideline, and the defensive back was headed right for the sideline, and the guy never touched him."

Womack had been a backfield mate in high school with James Brooks, a great back at Auburn. But like a lot of great high school running backs, he discovered that he was better suited to be a blocking back. And he and Ronnie Stewart on that 1980 team were two of the best we ever had.

"I didn't miss blocks too often," Womack said, "but when I did, Herschel would never say anything."

The offensive linemen loved blocking for Walker.

"Absolutely," guard Tim Morrison said. "It is a confidence builder. You know that you just hold it for one or two steps, he is going to get out on the corner, and he's going to make it happen.

"The greatest thing is when you have an offensive guard who runs a 4.9 or 5.0 40 pulling out on the corner on a sweep, and a guy who runs a 4.3 40 taps you on the shoulder and says, 'Block him.' That's a great feeling. You know he's right here, and it tells you which way to go to hit the guy, and he's gone. It was quite an experience to block for a guy like that."

The other guard, Jim Blakewood, doesn't remember much about Walker's long run. He got knocked out in the game, but he played.

"The whole second half is a fog," Blakewood said. "I got knocked out, but I didn't know it. I felt like I was on cloud nine, like I had been put to sleep temporarily."

John Kasay noticed that Nat Hudson was helping Blakewood back to the huddle. He dispatched Warren Gray to get Blakewood out of the game, but he literally would not come out.

"Coach Kasay got real angry with Warren and sent him back in for me," Blakewood said. "I came to the sideline that time, but I convinced them that I was fine, and I played like that the whole second half."

TIM CROWE ALMOST MAKES THE SOUTH CAROLINA HIGHLIGHT REEL

George Rogers had a good game that day, and he certainly made an impression on one of our defensive linemen, Tim Crowe.

Crowe would later make a tackle in the Sugar Bowl that I called the hit of the decade, and people today still remind him of it.

"People come up to me today," Crowe said, "and say, 'That was a heck of a hit in the Sugar Bowl.' But all my friends remind me that they remember when George Rogers ran over me."

Crowe was impressed with Rogers from watching the film, and he had heard the talk that compared Rogers to Earl Campbell. And of course, he practiced every day against Walker.

"I can't compare George Rogers to Herschel," Crowe said. "There is a difference between a game and practice. I never really felt anything when I was playing a game.

"But George got me," Crowe admitted. "I remember the play. Their guard pulled, and I stepped into the tackle. I saw George running around the corner, and it was like slow motion. He reversed his field. I had done a split like a goalie. I had a tackle on me, and one leg way out, and he ducked his head and hit me. But his foot went into my facemask, and that is what tripped him up."

The next day when Erk Russell ran the film, he couldn't resist.

"That's the way to use your head, Timmy."

ANOTHER BIG FUMBLE RECOVERY

Rex Robinson kicked another long field goal later, and we had a 13-0 lead. But they rallied. They kicked a field goal in the middle of third quarter, and then they had a little scooter guy, Carl West was his name, and he went 39 yards for a touchdown. He just kept on going.

Rogers would fumble two more times in the game. The second one saved the game for us. We were losing the field position late, and we had a short punt that put them at our 47, and then came Rogers. Plus nine, plus three, plus eight, plus seven. All of a sudden they were on our 17-yard line.

Then Scott Woerner made another great play when he caused a fumble and Tim Parks recovered it. We called him "Seemore," and

**Tim Crowe was a huge hit with fans when his attempt to tackle
South Carolina's George Rogers was only successful because
Rogers's foot got snagged by Crowe's facemask.**
Photo by Perry McIntyre Jr.

I can still see him coming out of that pile with those big old eyes of his.

"I remember Pat McShea giving the first down, Georgia signal," Robert Miles added. "I also remember that we had to have a TV timeout during the game because I got laid out. For some reason, my mother was on the sideline for that game, and she didn't see a thing."

We almost didn't get out of the hole, but they roughed our punter, and we then drove all the way down to the one-yard line. They stopped us on fourth and one, but there were only 45 seconds left in the game.

Safety Jeff Hipp intercepted a desperation pass to clinch it for us.

"I tried my best to get into the end zone," said Hipp, who grew up in West Columbia, South Carolina, albeit a Clemson fan.

WERE THE HEISMAN VOTERS PAYING ATTENTION?

George Rogers won the Heisman Trophy that year. Of course, I am prejudiced, but I felt like Herschel Walker deserved it, and if you look at the statistics from that game, you could make a great case.

Rogers gained 168 yards on 35 carries and fumbled on the key drive. Walker gained 219 yards on 43 carries and broke a 76-yard touchdown run. And don't forget the scoreboard: 13-10, Georgia.

Of course, our players agreed.

"George was tough," Tim Crowe said. "But I can watch that game over and over, and Herschel had more yards and the long run, and George fumbled going in."

"I still contend that Herschel was the right candidate to win the Heisman that year," offensive guard Tim Morrison agreed. "George was instrumental in their program, but Herschel should have won the Heisman."

Of course, George Rogers was a senior and had an outstanding career. Walker was just a freshman, and the voters almost always use the test-of-time criteria, so I can understand Rogers winning it.

Chapter Ten

FLORIDA

THE FLORIDA GAME

O f all of the plays in Georgia's football history, the Buck Belue-to-Lindsay Scott touchdown that won the Florida game in 1980 is without a doubt the most important and the most significant. Not only for that game, but for what it led to, which was winning a national championship.

The Georgia–Florida game seemed to come down to one big play every year. That was true even before I came to Georgia.

I knew about the Georgia–Florida game from when I first started coaching. I went to the game for eight years to scout Georgia before they played Auburn. It was always the most fun game to scout of any that I scouted. You could get into the festivities of the occasion. I would even go to the breakfast for Georgia fans and then the Gator breakfast, too, and maybe get a little inside information. I would just ease into the pregame events and keep a low profile.

I remember in 1958 that Georgia just ran up and down the field and totally dominated the game but led 6-0. Florida was not even in the game, but they had one play, a long touchdown, and Florida won 7-6.

The next year was a conference championship season for Georgia, their last under Wally Butts, and the big play that year was a 100-yard interception return by Charley Britt, their safety. He went on to play for the Los Angeles Rams and landed a small role on the old *Ozzie and Harriet Show* as a fraternity brother to one of the Nelson boys.

My very first experience as a coach in the game in 1964 ended with a dramatic play. We were tied with Florida late in the game 7-7 and lined up for a field goal. We had a bad snap, but our kicker, Bobby Etter, who weighed 155 pounds, picked up the ball, scooted around the end, and dove backward into the end zone for a touchdown.

I remember 1975, of course, the famous Richard Appleby-to-Gene Washington end-around pass. In 1976, we were down two touchdowns at halftime and scored four unanswered touchdowns in the second half after we stopped them on a fourth-and-two in their own territory. Johnny Henderson, whose father, Billy, coached my sons in high school football at Clarke Central, made that tackle.

I remember 1981 when the score was the same as in 1980, but we had a long drive with Herschel Walker pounding out the yards. We won 44-0 in 1982, so that year was different, but I remember it. The 1983 game was when we marched 99 yards to win 10-9. And in 1985, Florida came in ranked No. 1 in the country, and we beat them 24-3. Keith Henderson and Tim Worley broke off long touchdown runs.

Of course, I remember the disasters, too. Most of the memories of the series are good ones, but I remember the bad ones.

The game really does have a bowl atmosphere. They were kind of lax about alcohol in previous years, so it came to be called the world's largest outdoor cocktail party. There were times that even on the field you could smell the alcohol.

COMPLICATED BY THE SCHEDULE

One of the things that made 1980 more of a challenge was that we were coming off the win over South Carolina, an emotional game. I knew it would be tough. Some years the problem was looking past our opponent the week before Florida. But it was just the reverse in 1980.

Plus, Florida had a daggone good football team. They were 6-1 and very much in the conference race. In fact, if they beat us, they would at least tie for the championship.

We got off to a good start when Walker went 73 yards for a touchdown on the fourth play of the game. It was a sweep, and I remember our tight end, Norris Brown, was blocking the guy eight, 10 yards down field. That was a testament to how well our receivers blocked.

"Nobody touched Herschel," receivers coach Charlie Whittemore recalled. "Norris Brown was blocking the defensive end 18 yards down the field. The guy can't get off him. And Lindsay Scott blocked the corner, and the corner did not touch Herschel."

Receivers like to catch the ball, but Charlie always tried to instill in them pride in blocking, too.

"We wanted three knockdowns," he said. "We wanted to knock a defender off his feet three times. That was a star. We had times when guys might get six to eight to 10 knockdowns."

Charlie told the receivers that the aggressive blocking would help his receivers catch more passes, too.

"That defensive back doesn't know if you are going to knock his feet out from under him or run by him," Charlie said.

HERSCHEL WALKER'S STAGE

When the game was over, Herschel Walker had gained 235 yards on 37 carries, but it was overshadowed by the dramatic comeback we made. Walker dominated the Gators like no other team.

"He was a different person for the Florida game," backfield coach Mike Cavan said. "He sensed the magnitude of that game. Go check his record. It is unbelievable. It's ridiculous."

The numbers support Mike's assertion. In three games against Florida, Walker rushed for 649 yards and scored eight touchdowns.

In 1981, Georgia beat Florida by an identical 26-20 score, but instead of a long play, we won it with a long drive. Walker carried the ball almost every play on the long drive. He scored all four of our touchdowns in that game.

"That game to him was big, huge," Mike exclaimed. "I remember in his last year down there, we were winning 44-0, and the whole fourth quarter the fans kept coming down to the fence. I thought they were going to come over the railing after him."

Accompanied by quarterback John Lastinger, Walker exited the field with half a quarter to play, simply for his own safety.

Most of the time when you score quickly like we did with Walker's long run in 1980, it can hurt you. I remember when we lost at Ole Miss in 1976. We had just shut out Alabama 21-0, and we threw a 75-yard touchdown pass to Gene Washington on our first possession and our quarterback Ray Golf had a long run on an option play for a touchdown. At that moment we thought we were the greatest team in America, and we wound up losing that game.

But we didn't relax in 1980 against Florida. In fact, we got ahead 14-3 before it got close.

SURPRISE! SURPRISE!

Bill Lewis and our secondary made a good team. He prepared them meticulously, and they were a smart veteran group of players.

"They played very sound fundamentally," agreed Bill, speaking of his defensive backs. "When you do that, you can make up for a certain lack of speed. Erk Russell had built a solid system, and we were able to adjust well. Plus Erk was unbelievable at being able to call the game and adjust to what people were doing."

Ordinarily, our defense was well prepared for what we played against. But Florida surprised us.

"Remember," Bill said, "they had Mike Shanahan as their offensive coordinator. Florida was making the transition to Wayne Peace at quarterback. Peace had started his first game against Ole Miss just two weeks before, and Florida basically lined up with two tight ends and three backs and protected Peace. They handed the ball off, had a good kicking game, and won a close, low-scoring game."

That was the style of attack that we prepared for, but Florida surprised us.

"The first time they broke the huddle, they lined up with four wide receivers," Bill recalled. "They were using an early version of the Run and Shoot, throwing and catching."

"They were lining up with multiple receivers and doing some crossing routes and trying to pick us off," Jeff Hipp recalled. "It was something we had not really studied. That was the only game where we were not quite as prepared."

"They fooled us," Mike Fisher agreed. "They came out with those double wideouts, and we were just not prepared. We couldn't get Will Forts, one of our linebackers, to move himself out. The game plan was so thoroughly in his mind. People were hollering at him, and Frank Ros tried to push him into position."

"No one else in the league had an offense like that," Pat McShea said. "It was an offense that was ahead of its time. They hurt us pretty bad with those little, short passes."

"The weakness of the Split 60 is up the middle," Greg Bell explained. "It is good against the option. But the players we had were not the caliber of today's athletes. We didn't have the height or the speed. If you spread our guys out, we were in a bad position."

Florida had a great playmaker in Chris Collinsworth, and he scored a touchdown in the second quarter, beating Hipp on the play.

We also had four turnovers by halftime, including one by Walker. He didn't fumble much. Four turnovers—that right there can beat you.

MEET TYRONE YOUNG

Critical to the success that Florida enjoyed in that game was the play of a tall wide receiver named Tyrone Young. He was about six foot six, and he had an incredible day. I don't believe he had caught a pass all year before that game, which was why he was such a surprise. He caught 10 that day for 183 yards.

The biggest was a 54-yarder in the fourth quarter. That set up an 11-yard run by one of their tailbacks, and then he caught the two-point conversion. That made it 20-18 us about a minute into the fourth quarter.

Young frustrated our secondary all day with short passes, and frustration can lead to mistakes.

"I remember I screwed up," Greg Bell said. "I was the right cornerback, five yards off the line. Wayne Peace makes his three-step drop. Frank Ros is covering the inside guy, and Young has picked the inside guy."

Bell intended to put an end to Young's frustrating probes with a big hit.

"I was going to break this guy in half," he said. "He was as thin as a pencil."

Bell dropped his head and left his feet. But at the same time, Frank Ros got there and spun him around. Bell flew by him like a missile. Jeff Hipp was somewhere else, and there went Young for 54 yards.

Florida didn't go ahead until about halfway through the fourth quarter when they kicked a field goal to go up 21-20.

On our first attempt to rally, we were offsides on first down. Then Walker lost a couple and Belue threw two incompletions.

Florida was trying to kill time, so they ran the ball at us, and they made two first downs, but we finally stopped them and forced a punt. But there was only 1:35 left, and we had the ball on our own eight-yard line.

WE BLEW IT

As the game wound to what looked like its inevitable conclusion, our players on the sidelines maintained hope born of youthful optimism, but at the same time there was a feeling of having blown a tremendous opportunity.

Defensive guard Joe Creamons was from Eustis, Florida, and had attended many of the Georgia–Florida games in the 1970s. Some of his buddies took the opportunity to remind him of the mistake he had made in going to Georgia by flipping him a bird from beyond the fence.

"I remember feeling total disgust," Creamons said. "We had really outplayed Florida, but that game had gotten away from us. I couldn't believe we were going to lose to those guys."

"I remember they announced that Georgia Tech had tied No. 1 Notre Dame," Jeff Hipp said. "We were No. 2. I could just see the dream being shot down."

"We were all pretty depressed," Greg Bell said. "The defense lost that game. We screwed up. You could have dug a hole and put us all in it."

The malaise seemed common among the defensive backs.

"I felt like we had blown our undefeated hopes," Bob Kelly said. "All of us on defense were standing there thinking we had really let this one slip away."

Receiver Anthony Arnold, sidelined in that game with an injury, was the eternal optimist. He was on the sidelines icing his ankle, listening to television reporters give an update about Tech's 3-3 tie with Notre Dame.

"I never feel like I lost," he said. "Maybe I just ran out of time. I always thought we had a chance. Even in the Florida game, I never gave up. I had already figured out that we were going to go down the field and kick a field goal."

Rex Robinson had demonstrated earlier in his career that he could make clutch kicks. In 1978, he kicked the game-winning field goal up at Kentucky after he had missed two earlier in the game.

Pat McShea was somewhere between hopeful and hopeless.

"I had not completely given up, but I was not feeling too good. It was looking real doubtful," he said.

"The Florida game should never have gotten to where it was," linebacker Frank Ros agreed. "They did not belong on the same level as Tennessee. We made an All-American out of Tyrone Young that year."

Ultimately, Herschel Walker became an excellent pass receiver as well, but we had not developed that facet of getting the ball to him yet. We didn't want to burden him too much with anything other than running the ball.

But running the ball was a low-percentage risk that late in the game, effectively taking away Walker as a threat. Yet he, too, remained hopeful.

"It was weird," he recalled. "We were at our own goal line, but I didn't think that we were going to lose that game. I don't think anyone on the sideline thought we were going to lose."

Jim Broadway, who had started the year as the punter but was now just the holder on placekicks, shared Walker's hope.

"It sounds a little corny," he said, "but we found ways to win that year. If you go back and look at the stats, we didn't blow people away, but we had a sense we were not going to lose, and it all emanated from the Tennessee game."

Squab Jones, our longtime manager, was mumbling, but Hugh Nall, our injured center, was talking up our hopes.

"It ain't over; it ain't over yet," Nall kept saying.

"Squab was the only negative I heard," Nall added. "Everybody else still believed. I just _knew_ we weren't going to lose that game."

We didn't do anything on the field the first two plays to encourage hope. Belue lost a yard on the first play, and we dropped a pass on the second one.

THE PLAY

So it was third and 11, but to center Joe Happe, it felt like it was "third and a million" when he crouched to snap the ball. Robin Fisher, Florida's nose guard, looked him in the eye and said, "We are going to the Sugar Bowl."

Happe didn't respond. He just blocked Fisher for all he was worth.

The play was 76.

We would take our flanker, and he would run a skinny post through the middle. The tight end would drag across, and the split end would run the hash route.

A variation of the play had nearly worked the series before when Buck Belue threw to Chuck Jones, the flanker opposite Lindsay Scott.

"There was an opening between the safety and the corner and Buck almost got it there then," receivers coach Charlie Whittemore said. "But the Florida defensive backs misdirected the ball just a little. If Chuck had made that catch, he would have scored, because both defenders fell down."

We were not thinking about a touchdown. What was important was to get a first down and get out of the hole.

Lindsay Scott's first touchdown reception of 1980 was a 93-yarder that clinched a 26-20 comeback win over Florida with a minute left to play. *Photo by Randy Miller*

"All we wanted was to get close enough so Rex could kick a field goal," guard Tim Morrison said.

Belue took the snap and rolled first to his left, but the Florida defense collapsed on him, so he reversed his field and went to the right. Nat Hudson delivered a key block that gave him some time, keeping an onrushing end away from the quarterback.

"I went after the rusher," Hudson said. "I knew I had to do something."

Before Belue threw the ball, he pointed for Scott to slide a little to his left.

"I had run a deep curl-in, but when Buck pointed, I slid over to a dead spot in the zone," Scott said.

Buck passed it to Scott at the 25.

When Scott first caught the ball, my first thought was, "We got it!" We had the first down, but then he hit the ground running and took off. "I was thinking like everybody else," Scott said. "We have an All-America kicker. I knew I had the first down. But it just broke. Once I turned up field, I don't think they expected that. I came down and that initial burst got me going. I just outran them."

He came along the sidelines, and I outran him for 10 yards, and then he passed me.

"I was just flat running," Scott said. "I was expecting to get hit when I caught it. After that, instinct takes over. There was not a whole lot of time to think about it. I knew I had to do something."

"It was almost like Lindsay had wings on his feet," Morrison remembered. "I could only see the back end of everything. I collapsed at midfield on top of Buck. I was done, spent. The emotional strain, the physical strain, it all becomes evident at the end of the game."

Happe couldn't get off his knees.

"There was a crowd on the field, and I couldn't see but the upper half of Lindsay. I just kept saying, 'Go, go, go.'"

From his viewpoint, Happe knew Scott had scored only by the reaction of the Georgia spectators.

Hudson didn't have a good viewpoint either.

"To be honest, I was working too hard," he said. "I knew by the roar of the crowd that something was happening, but I was thinking that we had a chance for a field goal."

Cornerback Greg Bell was sitting dejectedly on the sideline when the roar of the crowd brought him to the sidelines.

"I was looking down the sideline, and I saw Erk Russell," Bell said. "He looked at me and said, 'That was something, wasn't it?' I can still see his expression. He looked at it like it was an everyday event."

On the tape, you can see center Hugh Nall on crutches on the sideline, running down the field as Scott scores.

"I've got the fastest time in the 50-yard dash on crutches," Nall laughed. "I left the 50 and sprinted and jumped on that pile when Lindsay Scott scored that touchdown. If you watch the film, you can see a one-legged guy, and I was kicking it.

"Everybody ran down there about as fast as Lindsay did," Tim Crowe chuckled. "It was like a bunch of ants. If you look at the replay, you can see Jeff Harper in the pile, swinging his fists like crazy. That corner of the end zone was Bulldog heaven."

While many of the players were running down the field chasing Scott, Bob Kelly ran out on the field to tackle quarterback Buck Belue.

"I put the best tackle of my career on Buck at the 50," he said. "I just hammered him. I didn't let him up for about a minute."

PERSONAL REDEMPTION

That play has followed Lindsay Scott all his life. People always want to talk to him about that play.

"People want to know what I was thinking at that moment, what was going through my mind," he said. "They want to feel like they were part of it.

"To a lot of people, it is the greatest play in Georgia's history. A lot of people remember the Munson call. It all goes hand in hand."

It was also a personal redemption for Scott, who had endured a difficult six months. His scholarship had been suspended after an altercation with a counselor at the dorm. He had wrecked his car and been told he would never play football again. And he had seen his role diminish on a team that had discovered a great tailback. He'd only caught 11 passes before that game, and none for a touchdown.

In fact, a story had been published in the paper earlier in the season that he and Anthony Arnold were not satisfied with their roles in the offense.

I called them into my office and basically showed them the door.

"I believe we have won a few ballgames before you got here," I said.

Two weeks later, Scott was late for a team meeting, and he was demoted to second team.

"That moment in the Gator Bowl did so much for me as far as my confidence and as far as getting myself back on the right track, back in the right mode where I should have been," Scott explained.

"That moment going down the sidelines was like a ton of pressure came off my shoulders. My career took a jump for the better after that play."

There was not a lot of time for thinking as Scott ran down the field, but he clearly recalls his first thoughts after he scored.

"You have to remember that I played for Vince Dooley," Scott said. "My first thought was, 'I hope there are not any flags.' Well, maybe my first thought was how excited I was, but the second one was, 'Lord, don't let there be any flags.'"

There Was a Flag

There was a penalty, and I was mad when I saw that flag come out. Bobby Gaston was the referee. I've known him a long time. He came up to me and told me that they were going to flag us for excessive celebration.

"How much?" I asked.

"Fifteen yards," he said.

With a chuckle, Gaston later reminded me what I said.

"Well, that seems a little excessive."

Up in the Press Box

I was not aware of it at the time, but we almost lost our offensive coordinator up in the press box.

Although the 93-yard touchdown pass from Buck Belue to Lindsay Scott may be the most famous play in Georgia football history, our offensive coordinator George Haffner did not even see Scott score.

In fact, linebackers coach Chip Wisdom said George nearly fell out of the Gator Bowl press box.

"I saved George's life," Chip laughed.

When the pass from Belue to Scott turned into a long game-saving touchdown, the Georgia coaches in the press box naturally reacted with excitement, jumping and cheering as Scott raced for the goal line. In the excitement, George's headset fell off. Instinctively, he leaned forward to grab the headset, which was clipped to his clothing and would not have fallen far anyway.

But George lost his equilibrium and leaned forward over the press box facing.

"The press box then seemed like it was about 10 stories up, hanging way out over the fans," Chip recalled.

Recruited together even though they came from different high schools, quarterback Buck Belue of Valdosta and Lindsay Scott of Jesup dreamed of making game-winning plays like the 93-yarder that beat Florida in 1980. *Photo by Wingate Downs*

"So George leaned out the press box to catch his headset, and both his legs came up, and George was slipping out," Chip remembered. "As Lindsay was scoring, I reached out and grabbed his belt.

"I always tell people it was an offensive coach doing what an offensive coach does, and a defensive coach reacting with instinct like a defender. He was thinking that he needed to be able to communicate with his offense, and I was reacting on instinct."

Chip adds one other note.

"I have to say this," he said. "I saw Lindsay score with my peripheral vision."

MEANWHILE, BENEATH THE STANDS

Barbara went to the game, but she did not sit in the stands. This was just a few weeks after the automobile accident after which her spleen had ruptured. So it was arranged for her to watch the game in a trailer that was parked underneath the stadium. They assured her that she would be alright to travel.

Her brother, Johnny, was there, too. He is one of those people who can be the biggest fan or the worst football critic. He was up in the stands, but he came down at a time when it looked like we were finished, and he just laid into Barbara about what a sorry coaching job I was doing. And then he left.

About that time the place went crazy, and he ran back in bragging about how I did such a heck of a coaching job. Ironically, Johnny's daughter, Laney, later married Mike Bobo, a quarterback and a coach at Georgia.

Barbara said she will always remember a Florida fan in the parking lot just flinging his radio to the ground when we scored.

GREAT TASTE

There was still more than a minute to play after Lindsay Scott's touchdown, time for a Run and Shoot offense to drive for a touchdown of its own. But Mike Fisher, who grew up in Jacksonville as a fan of the Gators and vowed he would never play with those rednecks at Georgia, intercepted a pass on Florida's first play and ran it back 25 yards.

Fisher's afternoon had started off on the wrong foot. One of the Florida cheerleaders was a girl he had dated in high school. During the course of warming up, he had chatted with her briefly.

Secondary coach Bill Lewis interrupted the encounter.

"Mike, do you think maybe we can get you involved on the field out here? Maybe catch a few punts?"

Three and a half hours later, after all the ups and downs of an incredible college football game, Bill told Fisher, "Great taste."

"Huh?"

"In girls. Great taste in girls."

FIRST, RELIEF

The first emotion we all felt was relief.

"I think back to when Florida was third and 10, and we had to make a stop," Frank Ros said. "If we don't bone up then, they run the clock out. That was definitely one game that never should have gotten to the point it did."

"Here was our chance to be No. 1, and we almost blew it," Chris Welton said. "I knew we had matured as a team. It was our biggest win ever in terms of last-minute heroics that we had ever been a part of. But after the big celebration in the end zone, in the locker room you could have heard a pin drop. The realization was setting in that we had almost blown the thing. We figured we were going to get chewed out for playing so poorly in the second half."

What the players saw was what they called the well-known stare.

"Well, hell! We won the damn game!" I finally said.

That relieved the tension in the air, and the celebration started.

THEN, CELEBRATION

Not all the fans were in Jacksonville. There were still many in Athens, and they came to the dorm that night to help the players celebrate.

"We had a few kegs in the room," admitted Pat McShea, and to hear him tell it, it was almost the undoing of safety Jeff Hipp.

"Jeff almost died, I swear," McShea recalled. "He was up on the second floor leaning over the railing when he slipped and fell over the rail. Somebody reached out and grabbed his ankle and held on."

"Before I knew it, I had gone over the rail," Hipp admitted. "I was able to hang on with one hand until they were able to drag me back over. There are certain things you would like to forget, but that is one thing I don't think I will ever forget."

THEN, RESOLVE

"The Florida game is where we were born as a team," Herschel Walker said. "We had won some games and done some good things, but we were tested in that game. From then on, we didn't think we were going to lose."

Offensive line coach John Kasay agreed. On the plane ride home, he turned to Wayne McDuffie and said, "We are going to win them all now."

"That was the adrenaline we needed," John later said. "That game gave us the confidence that we could come back and do what we do best to win."

"After we beat Florida, we knew we could be special," Jeff Harper said.

Chapter Eleven

AUBURN

No. 1 on the Charts

Georgia Tech's 3-3 tie of Notre Dame knocked the Fighting Irish out of the No. 1 spot, and for the first time in my career, Georgia was ranked No. 1 in the nation.

But my mind was all on Auburn. Being ranked No. 1 could be a distraction. It was certainly not anything that I was excited about. It could have put more pressure on us. It was clear that we could win all of our games, but we had a tough road.

Auburn was going through a tough year. They were 5-4, and all four of those losses were conference losses. But I knew the history of this series better than any. Time after time, there were championships riding on it.

I remember when I was on the Auburn side as an assistant in 1959 when Georgia beat us 14-13 to win their last championship under Wally Butts.

I remember the Georgia punter kicking the Georgia fullback in the fanny with the football. The ball rolled all the way to the one-yard line, and Auburn recovered it and scored.

We had the game won late, we being Auburn. Brian Harvard was our quarterback. We wanted him to roll out on a pass play with the instruction don't throw the ball. He was out there flashing the ball, and he got hit, and Pat Dye recovered for Georgia. That set up the winning touchdown drive.

Of course, Georgia fans remember that Fran Tarkenton threw a touchdown pass to Bill Herron on a fourth-down play, and Durwood Pennington kicked the extra point that enabled Georgia to win. It was a disaster for me at the time, but it became a point of pride later as I became a Bulldog.

All three of the previous Southeastern Conference championships we had won at Georgia, in 1966, 1968, and 1976, had been clinched at Auburn. Of course, the veterans on the 1980 team had a chance to win the conference titles in 1978 and 1979. In 1978 we tied 22-22. And in 1979 they beat us.

That was the year the Sugar Bowl was really sweating it out. We came into the Auburn game with a 5-4 record, but we were 5-0 in the conference. If we tied Alabama in the standings, which was unbeaten and ranked No. 1 in the country, the rules at the time said that the Sugar Bowl had to take Georgia, because Alabama had been to the bowl more recently than we had.

Auburn beat us 33-13. Buck Belue broke his ankle very early in the game. Of course, the Sugar Bowl was still sweating bullets when Auburn and Alabama played. If Auburn somehow upset Alabama, we would still be tied for the conference title, and they would still have had to take us. I remember sitting in the press box with Sugar Bowl officials at the Auburn–Alabama game, and they were about to die because Auburn was rallying.

Alabama won, and the Sugar Bowl got the conference to change the rule the next year.

The fact that I had gone to school at Auburn might have meant something extra in the early years that I was at Georgia, but that diminished over time. There was just always so much riding on the game other than the fact I graduated from Auburn.

One of our most bitter losses ever was in 1971 when both teams were unbeaten coming into the game. That 1971 team was a great team. We had Andy Johnson at quarterback, and Jimmy Poulos playing tailback. Our defense was one of our best ever, with Chip Wisdom at linebacker, Chuck Heard at defensive tackle, and Mixon Robinson at defensive end. We had given up 25 points to Oregon State in the opener, and then in the next eight games combined, we gave up four touchdowns.

But Auburn beat us 35-20 with Pat Sullivan throwing to Terry Beasley. We helped Pat Sullivan win the Heisman Trophy. That team ended up 11-1 after, of all things, a 7-3 win in the Gator Bowl over North Carolina, which was coached by my brother, Bill. That was the first and last time we ever coached against each other, and I am glad of that, because it was hard on the family. The 1971 team finished the season ranked seventh in the country, but that one loss to Auburn was a bitter pill to swallow.

VOICE FROM THE PAST

The Auburn game has always been the most difficult to coach because it followed the Florida game and its bowl-like atmosphere.

If we beat Florida, we had to try to get the Georgia players back down to earth. You couldn't even *think* about getting the Georgia fans back down.

"You try to leave the last game behind," rover Chris Welton said, "but you couldn't avoid the events of the Florida game."

With us being No. 1, I didn't want the players to be overconfident. They shouldn't have needed any motivation, because we had not beaten Auburn in three years. But I didn't want to take any chances. So I brought in Frank Sinkwich to talk to the team.

Frank won the Heisman Trophy in 1942 when Georgia went to the Rose Bowl. But they were not unbeaten that year. They lost to Auburn 27-13.

"He told us how they beat Florida 75-0," tackle Tim Crowe said. "He said they were a 100-point favorite, and they went to play Auburn sky high."

"They kicked our butts," Frank told the team. "Don't think you won't remember it the rest of your life. It might slip out of your thoughts for a few years, but it will come back to you that you had a chance."

"Auburn was the hardest game to get ready for," Pat McShea agreed. "My whole career, they were the one team that screwed up the season. That tie in 1978 hurt."

ANOTHER SULLIVAN,
ANOTHER BEASLEY

It was just a strange coincidence that the younger brothers of Pat Sullivan and Terry Beasley were playing for Auburn that year. Joe Sullivan was their starting quarterback, but we actually saw a lot of their backup, Charles Thomas. And Jerry Beasley was a defensive back instead of a receiver.

The person we were really worried about was James Brooks, their tailback. Auburn had had the greatest bunch of running backs during that era: Brooks, Joe Cribbs, and William Andrews. Brooks had already rushed for 1,146 yards before that game.

The first quarter was scoreless. Auburn scored first in the second quarter after a 91-yard drive. We answered with a field goal, but what really broke it open for us was a blocked punt that Freddie Gilbert returned for a touchdown. I can still see Greg Bell coming off the corner. He had good speed, so that was one reason he was there. And Gilbert had big hands. I can see those long legs running down the field.

THE ANATOMY OF A BLOCK

Greg Bell still has a photo of his blocked punt in his office. The odd thing is that he had only been in that rush end position for a couple of weeks.

Until the Florida game, he had been one of the upbacks on the punt return team. He and Bob Kelly and Mike Fisher made a wedge, and their goal was to give Scott Woerner just enough room to break out.

But somebody got hurt the week before. I think it was Dale Carver, so Erk Russell was looking for volunteers to rush, and Bell volunteered.

Bell had been paying attention to Chip Wisdom's instructions of how to rush, and he almost blocked a punt against Florida. He went over the up back and landed on the punter. So it was not a surprise to us that he blocked it.

"We came out flat against Auburn," Bell recalled. "We had just played a big emotional game. Auburn was not having a good season, but they came out like they did every year against us, playing like All-Americans."

It was not until Auburn's third punt of the game that Bell blocked the kick, but he set it up with some clever alignment on the first two punts.

"By the time the line would come out and line up," Bell explained, "I was already on my knee, lined up. The first time I was way outside of the guy on the line."

He put on a burst of speed and rushed around the blocker, but to no apparent effect.

"The whole thing Coach Wisdom had talked about was to get the guy to move his inside foot," Bell said. "Everybody was blocking an area, so you had to leave your inside foot in place or you change the whole spectrum of the line. I was trying to get him to move his inside foot, which he did, because he had to come way outside to get me."

On the second Auburn punt, Bell once again dropped to a knee before Auburn came to the line, but this time he had carefully positioned himself over the blocker's outside shoulder. Bell used the same outside rush strategy, again drawing the blocker wide.

"The third time he came out, I was already on a knee," Bell said. "But I was lined head up on him, but he didn't notice it. He was getting tired, and the game was going on. This time I took a jab step to the right, and sure enough, he moved his inside leg, and I was able to get inside."

Greg Bell blocks a punt by Auburn's Alan Bollinger in Georgia's 31-21 win that clinched the SEC title. The coach kicking in the background is Auburn's head coach Doug Barfield.

The upback was caught looking to the right, and Bell got in there cleanly for the block.

"We had a punt return called that play," Bell recalled. "If I had missed, I would have been cussed out. It was a risk."

Most of the defense was peeling back to block on the return, so it wasn't until they heard the thud of the ball that they knew the ball had been blocked.

"It changed the tone of the game," Bell said.

After the point after, Bell huddled with the kickoff team around assistant coach Bill Lewis.

"He was not one of those in-your-face guys," Bell said. "But he was always so serious. In that huddle before the kickoff, he was just looking at me and looking at me."

Bell broke the tension.

"Well, hell, somebody had to do it."

THE STORY BEHIND THE PHOTO

A month later, Greg Bell was in the hallway of the Georgia Coliseum when a member of the track team complimented him on the great season.

"Oh, by the way," he added, "that is one of the best pictures I've ever seen of someone blocking a punt."

That got his attention immediately, because every photo he had seen up to then had been taken from the press box, the style of the day, showing a progression of the play.

"There was not one good photo," he said. "I had been depressed about the whole thing."

But there was a photo published in Opelika, Alabama, which was taken from the Georgia side of the field. It showed Bell laid out and the ball popping up.

"The best thing was Doug Barfield, the Auburn coach, in the background, kicking," Bell said.

CLOCK PLAY! CLOCK PLAY!

We had made it a habit that year of scoring touchdowns very late in the half, but we scored so late in the half against Auburn that it was almost part of the halftime show.

We started from our own 42 with about three minutes to go. Buck Belue made a nice 17-yard run to get inside the 20. With 16 seconds to go, Auburn was called for pass interference in the end zone, so that gave us a first and goal at the Auburn one-yard line, but with only nine seconds to go and no timeouts.

I don't remember what play we had called, but Belue fumbled the snap. But he had the presence of mind to call out "clock play, clock play," which was a fade to the tight end Norris Brown in the corner. So there was no time showing on the clock when the officials signaled touchdown. Belue did a great job of lining the play up.

Well, Paul Davis, the Auburn defensive coordinator, ran out on the field complaining that time had expired before we snapped the ball. Even though it was halftime, they flagged him 15 yards for unsportsmanlike conduct. He was madder than hell.

Well, with us kicking off from the Auburn 45 to start the second half, it was an easy decision to go for an onside kick, and Will Forts recovered it. Belue made another good run, a 26-yard scramble, and we scored again to go up 24-7.

Buck Belue played one of his best games against Auburn.

That was one of Belue's best games. Herschel Walker was held to 77 yards on 27 carries. Belue had 77 yards on just nine carries, and he completed 10 passes for 99 yards.

Belue did everything good, nothing sensational. He was not real strong or fast, but he did everything well. He could scramble. He could throw on the run. He was solid, smart, experienced. He had played a lot of football before he got to Georgia. He was a starter at Valdosta High for a long time.

The players respected Belue, and that is the thing you are constantly looking for above anything else. He was a competitor, and he had to learn when he got here that you don't take this whole thing on yourself. You have weapons. Use your weapons. If you get in a bad situation, don't try to do it all yourself. He finally got to the point where he understood there are going to be some bad plays, and he could come back and get them on the next play.

He got to be a total quarterback by relying on the total offense. I think the greatest tribute to him is that he is the only quarterback in Georgia's history to have won SEC championships back to back.

ANOTHER CHAMPIONSHIP ON THE PLAINS

All but one of the six SEC championships we won were won in even-numbered years, when we played at Auburn, so we clinched five of them at Auburn, and 1980 was no exception.

Herschel Walker did not have a great game that day, but he did score a touchdown on an 18-yard run in the third quarter that put us ahead 31-7. Auburn came back with two long drives, but they never really threatened us. We got down to the Auburn two-yard line and threw an interception, and then we were on the Auburn seven-yard line when the game ended.

We came home with a 31-21 win and a conference championship.

Chapter Twelve

GEORGIA TECH

DON'T LET HISTORY REPEAT ITSELF

None of the teams I had coached at Georgia had ever gotten to the Georgia Tech game with a perfect record. The 1966 team lost down at Miami by one point in the middle of the season. The 1968 team had not lost, but it had two ties. The 1971 team was the one that lost its next-to-last game against Auburn. To their credit, they made one of the most incredible comebacks a Georgia team has ever made to win at Georgia Tech on Thanksgiving night. And the 1976 team had lost at Ole Miss.

But two times in Georgia's history, Bulldog teams had indeed reached the last game against Georgia Tech with a perfect record. The 1946 team that featured Charlie Trippi was 9-0 when it beat Georgia Tech 35-7 and went on to beat North Carolina 20-10 in the Sugar Bowl.

But the 1927 team was 9-0, too. Only three teams had scored on Georgia that year. Among their wins that year was a 14-10 decision at Yale, and that was a big win in those days. That Georgia team was ranked No. 1 by two polls and poised to go to the Rose Bowl as the national champions, except it lost 12-0 in the season finale at Georgia Tech.

Tech had a good team in 1927. They did not have a good team in 1980. It was Bill Curry's first year, and they came in 1-8-1. But I did not want us to overlook them. I did not want history to repeat itself.

So we asked a man named Harvey Hill who had been on that 1927 Georgia team to come over and speak to the team. He was good because he remembered that 1927 game. He remembered how it cost them the national championship so he was really fired up and gave a great talk.

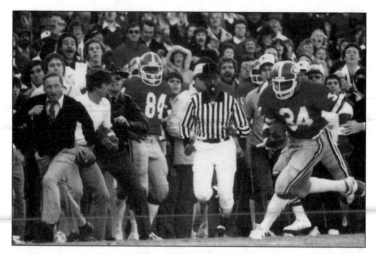

As Herschel Walker skirted the end on Georgia Tech, I was right there with him. This run broke Tony Dorsett's record for rushing yards by a freshman in a single season.

NEVER HAD A CHANCE

Even though Georgia Tech had helped us rise to No. 1 with its 3-3 tie of Notre Dame, Bill Curry's team never really had much of a chance that day. The big thing I remember about the game is Herschel Walker's run that broke the game open and also broke Tony Dorsett's freshman rushing record.

I had not really given the record any thought. Whatever would be would be. I was excited and happy when he did it. He made a long run that broke the game open and broke the record.

He was stopped at the line of scrimmage. Tech had him. They were bunched up, and he just, whoosh, left them.

Tech had just had a long drive from its own 14-yard line to close it to 31-21 with most of the fourth quarter still to play. You know, with a score like that the game is in doubt. But they put all of that effort into that long drive, and then in one play, we got the seven back, and that deflated them.

FAREWELL TO THE TRACKS

The Tech game was also the last game for the fans on the railroad tracks.

Sanford Stadium was built into a natural valley. The railroad built a trestle and an embankment on the east end of the stadium, across the road from the stadium. For many years, it was a way for spectators to see the games for free.

It was a pretty good distance from the field, but the perspective gave a good view of the whole field. The better our teams did and the greater the sale of tickets, the higher the demand to sit on the tracks, too.

Of course, the rules were a little more lax on the tracks, particularly with regard to alcohol. So they were usually in a very good mood.

After we announced that the stadium was going to be expanded, a handful of students identifying themselves as tracks fans came in with a petition. They were very serious and were doing a great sales job. Their main selling point was that this was a great tradition, that they were known all over the United States.

There was no denying it was a great tradition. Of course, they were seeing the game for free.

We always transported the players by bus from our football locker room in the Coliseum over to the stadium, where they exited the bus directly in front of the fans on the tracks. It always gave us a huge boost before the game. It probably helped us recruit some players, too. They were awestruck when they got off that bus and saw the reaction of those people.

Probably the greatest moment ever for the fans of the tracks was the Alabama game in 1976. They started staking out their spots as early as Wednesday.

I came by there Friday night before the Alabama game. At 7 p.m. there was not a place left that anybody could sit down. Even those down on the streets had a seat, and they couldn't even see the field, but they were partying, right on up to the top.

What happened eventually was someone fell down and got hurt. So we really needed a way to address the safety issue.

I remember that they were throwing things at the opponents' buses, so we had to appeal to them. The next game they all had marshmallows that they threw. They were able to understand and adjust but still be creative.

Some of the players on the 1980 team made their official visit the day we beat Alabama, and the tracks fans might have had something to do with them coming to Georgia.

"The hair on the back of my neck still stands up when I think about stepping off the bus at the Georgia–Alabama game in 1976 with Erk Russell," Tim Morrison said. "The feeling I got sold me on the program.

The crowd on the railroad tracks watched the game for free until 1981 when the expansion of the stadium blocked the view.

"When they closed the end zone, they lost a lot. What a great group of people!"

"You could go out there on Wednesday or Thursday and people had put their stuff out there," Nat Hudson marveled. "The next day you might see a tent or a mattress, and then lawn chairs or sofas and even recliners. They would be sleeping overnight.

"They showed up every week. They were going to be with you. No matter what, that group of fans was going to show up. I always worried about the train coming. I think they had the track blocked at both ends."

"I talk about the tracks all the time," Lindsay Scott recalled. "The most fun time I had in Athens was when we got off those buses and those people up there went wild. If you couldn't get fired up from that, you couldn't get fired up."

The anticipation of the experience only served to magnify it.

"You come off that bus, and your hair would stand up," Tommy Thurson said. "If you could not be ready to play then, you could not get ready."

Marty Ballard experienced how the reaction could go the other way. That unbridled enthusiasm could turn if we played poorly, like we did in 1979 when we lost our homecoming game to Virginia 31-0.

"The Virginia game sticks out because I remember all of the people on the tracks flipping us off," Ballard said.

"Coach Russell loved the tracks," Tim Crowe added. "There was always a guy who was dressed like a dog with an 'S' on his chest. Coach Russell always talked about that guy. He would pick out one fan and say, 'That's who we are going to watch today.'

"After the Tech game, we came back and there was a woman was on the sidewalk, totally ripped, drunk."

"Looks like she had a swell day," Erk said.

"And she did until someone threw her off the bank," Crowe said with a smile. "She was a Tech fan."

We were selling out every game, so it made sense to expand the stadium, and the most logical expansion was to close in the east end zone. Of course, that would mean that the view from the tracks would be obscured. So the Tech game was the last game that they could see the game from there.

Some of the players got the idea to get some t-shirts made up and throw them to the tracks fans as they got off the bus.

"We all signed the shirts," Joe Happe said. "As we got off the bus, we threw them up on the tracks. They got a big kick out of that. It was really an occasion when we did something for the fans. It was pretty neat."

The players' resources were limited. They did not print special shirts. They simply used markers to write on the shirts and to sign them.

"No one had any artistic talent," Pat McShea explained. "I remember after the season we were over at a place where we shouldn't have been and saw a couple of guys wearing them. We got a big kick out of that. It was pretty funny."

Robert Miles sat next to Herschel Walker on the bus ride over, and they traded shirts after they had signed them. The person who caught Miles's received a nice surprise, while the crowd that was trying to catch the one Walker threw must have been a little disappointed.

A PERFECT SEASON, SO FAR

Georgia Tech did not have a strong team in 1980, but that did not diminish the thrill of the 38-21 win. For one thing, you always want to beat your in-state rival. That game always means something extra to the players.

"I was happy that we clubbed Tech," John Kasay said. "I never liked Georgia Tech. That goes back to when I was a freshman. We used to go to the Capital City Club before the freshman game. I was the captain for the freshman game, and there were four of us who went to the club to represent the team, and we were totally ignored. They were slobbering all over them damn Georgia Tech players. We beat their ass 18-0, and I ain't never forgot it."

Of course, beating Georgia Tech gave us a perfect regular-season record, something we had not accomplished since I had been there. It looked like we could turn our full attention to the Sugar Bowl and beating Notre Dame for the national championship.

Chapter Thirteen

THE JOB OFFER

THE AUBURN JOB OPENS UP

After we finished the regular season 11-0, with a chance to win the national championship, it was probably quite shocking to many fans to see the headlines soon after the win over Georgia Tech that Auburn was trying to hire me as their head coach and that I was considering it.

Fob James, the governor of Alabama, started it. He was my roommate in college, and we had fished together a lot and stayed close. I was willing to listen when they called, and then it became more attractive.

Lee Hayley, who later came over to work in administration with me at Georgia, was the athletic director at the time, and he even said that he was willing to step aside and let me be the athletic director. They made a very attractive offer.

This happened right after the Georgia Tech game. In fact, that Sunday morning, I had a meeting with Erk Russell in the dorm. I told him I had this opportunity, and I wanted him to be aware of it. He was the first one to hear about it. If it came up, I didn't want him to be surprised. And if something happened that I did take the job, he was the one that I wanted to replace me.

I said, "Erk, you need to make plans to get the team ready to go to New Orleans, because I have to go take a look. If something happens, you need to be ready. They have made me an offer I can't ignore."

"You're kidding," said Erk, who was frankly shocked.

"No, I'm dead serious."

So that was how it was played out for a few days while I pondered the offer.

Of course, this shook a lot of people up, including the team. I didn't know what all was going through everybody's minds.

I was carried off the field after Georgia's 31-21 regular-season finale win over Georgia Tech in Sanford Stadium. *Photo by Fred Bennett*

The timing was certainly just as shocking as the possibility that I would leave Athens. The Heisman Trophy was announced that Tuesday morning, and ordinarily Herschel Walker's chance to win would have been the lead story on the sports pages. But it was kind of buried by this breaking news.

STAFF IS IN THE DARK

The rest of the coaching staff was just as surprised, and I guess I kept them in the dark.

"We were in the dark," agreed Chip Wisdom, Georgia's linebackers coach in 1980.

They learned from defensive coordinator Erk Russell that I was on my way to Auburn to interview for the football job.

"It seemed to me that we were left out in the cold," Chip said. "Not knowing was the worst torture of all. You get fired when you lose. You understand that."

But Chip said it was hard to process the fact that the staff could be on the brink of a national title and also unemployment, all at the same time.

Out of this uncertainty arose a concerted effort by the staff to push Erk as the preferred replacement for me if I did indeed leave Athens.

"Actually we heard that Vince had taken the job," Chip confessed.

At a staff meeting after it became accepted knowledge that I was going back to Auburn, Chip, as was his nature, spoke up.

"Guys, if I see this the way y'all see this, we all need to get on the same page," he said, "because right now, if Vince is gone, has he talked to any of y'all?"

Blank stares greeted him because Erk was the only one I had talked to.

"Then what I am hearing is that there is a move afoot to bring in Pat Dye," Chip continued. "Here we are on the verge of coaching a national championship team; if our head guy is going to Auburn and has not talked to all y'all about going with him, and he certainly hasn't talked to me, then where exactly does that put us?

"That being said we all need to get out and push Erk to be the head coach at Georgia. We need to be able to say as a staff we are either going to stay or not."

To a man the staff agreed. They began to compare notes with each other about who had a relationship with which trustee and which board member.

They could not rely on a public relations department to get the word out. The task was outside even the creative purview of a Dan Magill, the associate athletic director at Georgia who had been the school's sports information director.

"You might say that we were looking out for our own job security," Chip said.

So the staff mounted an in-house public relations campaign to fill the potential vacancy with Erk.

"We were all 100 percent in support of Erk being the head coach, and we could stay here with him," Chip confirmed.

Rumors always spring up in a situation like that. George Haffner was hearing things while he was out recruiting. An Alabama radio station contacted him to ask him what he thought about possibly coming to Auburn.

George had another reason for wanting to stick around. He had been at Pittsburgh under Johnny Majors in the mid-1970s, but he left the year before they won the 1976 national championship.

"My heart-and-soul goal was to get a national title," he said. "I had voluntarily left Majors and missed that opportunity. In my mind I was really fortunate to be in a position for this opportunity again. I wanted it bad."

"Being quite honest about it, we were more concerned about what was going to happen here," Mike Cavan admitted. "After we got over the surprise, we got behind Coach Russell, that he needed to get his affairs in line here and take this job. At that time, I didn't have any ideas about leaving. Our focus was what were we going to do about Georgia."

PLAYER REACTIONS VARY

I was not surprised by the reactions of the players, some of whom were upset, and some of whom seemed to take it in stride.

"It wasn't good timing at all," Greg Bell said. "We thought after we got through with Georgia Tech that we would be seeing headlines that this is the best Georgia team ever. But instead, it said, 'Dooley leaving, going to Auburn.'

"At first we were shocked. Then we thought it was just a rumor, and then it became truer and truer. Our first reaction was 'to hell with him.' It was like a betrayal. As you get older, you understand the politics, but not then. Here was one of the team members jumping off. We were offended."

"It unsettles any 18- to 20-year-old," Lindsay Scott said. "Here we were having the best season ever, going into a national championship game, and now we might not have a coach. That could rub some people wrong. Today, I understand. If you have a trump card, you have to play it."

"It was very weird," Chris Welton said. "In hindsight, you understand that a person had to look at his career in the context of his whole life, but for us, we had gotten to the most important games of our lives. How could he leave?"

The whole episode was over within just a few days, but the players quickly had realigned their priorities to win without me.

Jeff Hipp said the seniors made an effort to keep everybody level headed and focused on the job at hand.

"We had a great staff," Hipp said. "We still felt we were in good shape."

"More power to him," Anthony Arnold said. "In my mind, we were through with him."

"I would have been extremely disappointed," Bob Kelly said. "We had a close relationship, and I don't think many players did. In fact,

I don't know if there were a lot of players who liked him, because he was a little aloof and he was disciplinarian. I always thought he made the right call, except at Auburn in 1978. I was in his ear telling him to go for two."

DEEP ROOTS PREVAIL

In the end, I got back to Athens and looked at all of these pictures of Georgia players on the wall. All my children had grown up in Athens. When we drove to the airport to go over there, Derek was in the car crying. "I hate Auburn!" To him, Auburn was a big rival, and at that age it was all or nothing, love or hate.

I had coached in Athens for 17 years. If I had been here just five or six years, I might have jumped the Chattahoochee to go to Auburn. But I realized that my home was here. My roots were deeper in Athens, 17 years compared to eight as a coach and four as a player at Auburn, and more recent, too. So I couldn't leave. I had too much invested in Georgia. But I did listen, because there was some emotional pull.

The staff was relieved and glad to get back to work on preparing for Notre Dame.

"Everybody was totally professional about it," Chip Wisdom said. "We were focused on winning a national championship."

I think the players could have won without me anyway. If I had left them with Erk Russell in charge, they could have won it. But there had to be a little healing because there were some who couldn't understand how I could think about leaving them. It was hard for them to take, and I had to go back and explain so that they could understand.

I tried to explain to them that it was the fact that I had gone to school there, the fact that the governor was my roommate. I asked them to consider the fellow next to them, their roommate, in a similar position down the road. I had to try to paint them a picture. Once I did that, they accepted it better.

"It was like being recruited," Anthony Arnold said. "He goes on a fishing trip, and his buddy basically says, 'Name your price. Whatever it takes.' That is tough to turn down. I couldn't fault him for that."

"Will you have me back?" I asked the team.

"What are you going to say?" Chris Welton said. "But after one or two practices, it was forgotten."

GETTING IN SOME DIGS

The players got in one last good-natured dig before we played in the Sugar Bowl. Whenever we were practicing for a bowl game, we always had a Christmas party, and that year was no exception. That year the players had a little extra skit they dreamed up.

As a child, Greg Bell was impressed by comedians like Rich Little and Frank Gorshen who had mastered the art of doing impressions of famous people.

"I have an ear where I can pick up on people's dialects," he said. "I remember when I would get in trouble at home, I would change into John Wayne and that would catch my father off guard."

It didn't take Bell long at Georgia to notice the distinctiveness of my voice, and he learned to do a dead-on impression. The first time he revealed it was in 1978, near the end of the season.

In 1978, our season finale with Georgia Tech was aired by ABC. The day before the game, the players went to Sanford Stadium for their regular light walk-through routine and to do interviews with the network. Bell chose that day to reveal his impression of me.

Linebacker Danny Rogers and teammate Gordon Terry were walking just ahead of Bell, who called out in his best Dooley voice, "Rogers!"

Danny turned around, expecting to see me.

"Have you seen Coach Dooley?" he asked.

Naturally, this pleased Bell, and he did it again with Gordon Terry. That was when they found him out.

Bell's ability was like a new toy to his teammates, and they egged him on to do more. By the time they got to the field house, word was spreading among his teammates, who were clamoring for Bell to do more.

I had stayed on the field to do a television interview, so the players had a little extra time waiting for me to come in for a talk I did every week. Like all coaches, I was a little superstitious, so I tended to be a creature of habit about certain things. I had a big grease board that I would use to illustrate some key points to the players before games. As long as we were winning, I stuck to the same script.

"He wrote on the board the same thing before the game," Bell emphasized. "I had memorized the speech. We all had."

The players kept razzing Bell. Eventually, I'm told, they coaxed him up to the board, and he went into an impression of my regular talk. He wrote what I would normally start out with, "No mistakes."

"We don't need to make any mistakes," Bell said in my voice.

Of course, the players got a big kick out of this, and he kept going. He got through several of my points before one of their lookouts noticed that I was coming. So they erased everything and Bell got back into his seat. So I walk in, and it is very quiet, just the way I like it.

I pick up my marker, and I look around, and then I write No. 1, right over the top of where Bell had written it. "No mistakes."

As soon as I open my mouth, everybody starts laughing. Well, I snap around pretty quick, annoyed really, and it gets real quiet again.

So I write No. 2, and once again, without my noticing it, I'm going right over where Bell had written, and the rooms breaks up again. It is helter-skelter. Everybody couldn't stop laughing and talking.

"What the hell! What the hell is going on? Get control of your-selves!"

But the players were falling out. By the time I got to point three, I just said, "Hell, y'all know what to do, and you better do it tomor-row."

Later on I got an explanation that a player had been doing an impression of me. But I did not learn that it was Greg Bell until the Christmas party that year when an impromptu presentation show-cased his talent in front of me. I was good-natured about it, but Barbara just loved it.

During the trying 1979 season, when we struggled to a 6-5 record, Bell refused to lampoon me. The joke was not nearly as amusing on a 6-5 team as it had been on a 9-2-1 team.

Of course, the tenor of the 1980 season was much lighter, allow-ing for more levity. As the Christmas party neared, the players began to pester Bell to bring back his impression of me.

Finally, they invoked their bond as teammates, implying that Bell owed them this pleasure, and this was the last chance before they graduated. In 1978, he had done it solo, but this time he told them he was not going to be thrown under the bus alone.

Bell insisted that several of his teammates participate in the gag with him. I found out later that after practice, they spent about 20 minutes developing a brief skit. They would do an impression of a staff meeting. Bell would play my part. Offensive lineman Hugh Nall played Wayne McDuffie's role, for example.

"Everybody had a part," Bell explained. "Everybody did it impromptu. There were no scripts. We let it roll, and it was absolutely hilarious."

Bell came in dressed like me. He had a tie on, and he was trying to walk like I did, and he was carrying a suitcase with some orange and blue sticking out. He took off his dress shirt and underneath was an Auburn shirt.

"I'm not going to Auburn. I don't know where all those rumors are coming from," he kept saying.

It was a lot of fun. They were so accurate in their portrayal of a staff meeting that some of the trainers and managers caught some heat later for supposedly telling the players what went on in a staff meeting.

Bell said he gets requests all of the time from Bulldog clubs to come and do his impression, but he always refuses. We had a reunion of the 1980 team, and he did it then, but he has reserved it for team functions.

"I think the message is lost when you take it outside the house," Bell explained. "Plus, I don't think the general populace would understand the mannerisms."

ERK'S INEVITABLE DEPARTURE

The episode of my considering the Auburn job might have played a factor in Erk Russell leaving our staff that spring to start a new program at Georgia Southern.

Erk was not sure it reawakened anything in him, but it might have reawakened others to what a good head coach he would make.

"I always wanted to be a head coach," Erk said. "As I look back now, if you really want to be a head coach, you have to go about it a lot differently than I did then. I had the philosophy that somebody looking for a coach would check the resumé and say this guy would make a good head coach. It doesn't work that way. Maybe it does sometimes. But I don't think that people generally are going to come to you. There are too many people out there who want to look at the same opportunity who are more aggressive."

Erk has always said he was not even sure he would have gotten the job if I had gone to Auburn.

There were a lot of people on his side. He even had it from a reliable source that the athletic committee, which had to think ahead while I was considering the offer, felt the same way, but you never know.

"I don't think it could have worked out any better for me personally," said Erk, who started the program at Georgia Southern and won three Division I-AA national championships. "It couldn't have worked any better for me. But I'll always wonder what would have happened if Vince had gone to Auburn."

Chapter Fourteen

NOTRE DAME

THE NOTRE DAME GAME

When I was a boy growing up in Mobile, Alabama, Notre Dame was absolutely my favorite team. As a youngster, I would sit around a radio with a small group of boys, who were also Catholic, and listen to their games on the radio.

As a youngster, Notre Dame was where I wanted to go when I grew up. I said my prayers at night to go to Notre Dame. It was the aspiration of most Catholic boys who played football, all over the country. Notre Dame had that going for them. That was my school, and the one I wanted to go to.

They were under Frank Leahy then. They had Angelo Bertelli, Johnny Lujack, and Leon Hart, all Heisman Trophy winners. They had the tradition of Knute Rockne, but they were under Leahy then. They had some great teams.

Back in those days, it was almost an assumption that if you were from Notre Dame that you were a good coach. There was kind of an air about them. That is why so many Notre Dame coaches were hired. Frank Thomas had great success at Alabama. Harry Mehre came here to Georgia and had some success. But you also had Earl Brown, who didn't win a game at Auburn. It was just a perception they had in those days that if you were from Notre Dame, you knew how to coach.

That prevailed for a while before people like Bear Bryant at Alabama and Shug Jordan at Auburn came back to their alma maters and showed that they could win.

I never really considered scheduling Notre Dame for a regular game because we were in such a box with our schedule. We had eight conference games, and then we had to play Georgia Tech, a non-conference team, every year. That left only two games to play with, and we wanted to bring those two in Athens.

For years we could do that with teams like Oregon, Oregon State, California, Texas A&M, North Carolina State, Brigham Young, and UCLA. But we could not have done that with Notre Dame because we would have had to return the game.

Of course, Notre Dame was not well liked by most fans of Southern football, I suppose because of that aura the Fighting Irish project. So our fans were anxious to play them.

Some of our players shared the same excitement of playing Notre Dame. Our captain, Frank Ros, had grown up a Catholic like I had, and he was thrilled to play them. It was a big deal to Joe Happe, who had come from Pennsylvania where they have as many Catholic high schools as they do public high schools.

In fact, our first offensive play of the game, Joe Happe lined up at center, and their nose guard, Joe Gramke from Cincinnati, called Happe a redneck.

Happe looked at him and said, "Buddy, you are more of a redneck than I am. I'm from Pennsylvania."

GETTING AN EARLY JUMP

Notre Dame still had one more game to play against Southern Cal after our season was over. So we sent John Kasay out to Los Angeles to get a head start on breaking down film and to see them in person. It is always an advantage to see a team live.

But Notre Dame had an advantage that they were still playing a week later than we were, so we would have a longer break before the final game and more of a chance to get rusty.

John went out there and started to work on the scouting report. Coaches who scout other teams usually subscribe to out-of-town newspapers and read them throughout the season to get a better idea of who the key players are. We didn't have a subscription to any papers on Notre Dame, but they sent us some anyway.

"They were so arrogant that they wanted you to read everything about them," John explained. "They sent me a bundle of Sunday papers, and I sat there and read every one of them and wrote notes."

John was using a system he learned from Eddie Crowder, who was head coach at Colorado in the early 1970s. They met at the national coaching convention in 1971. John quizzed him on how he recruited. Crowder had a limited recruiting budget, so he used to order newspapers from all over the country. He paid people to read the local sports pages. They were to write down every name they saw and then put checks by it when those names were repeated.

"After a few weeks, he had a list of 30 or 40 of the guys whose names were mentioned most often," John said. "Those were the guys he contacted. He would write personal notes. He got the best players, and he saved a ton of money on recruiting."

John used the same system in scouting Notre Dame, and he was very impressed by what he saw.

"All those guys at Notre Dame were on the National Honor Society," he said. "They were not a bunch of dummies. That really impressed me about those guys. I asked our players to imagine how much less time they had to spend to teach something to a defense that has eight National Honor Society guys playing for it. They were smart as hell."

FOOD POISONING

We practiced in Athens before we let the players take a little break to go home for Christmas. Joe Creamons decided that instead of going all the way down to Eustis, Florida, and then coming back, that he would spend the holidays with Tim Crowe in nearby Stone Mountain.

The Crowes served spaghetti on Christmas Eve, but at about 2:30 a.m., Creamons woke up in so much pain that the Crowes had to take him to the hospital. His pain got so bad that they even administered morphine. He went from about 248 pounds to about 233 in a very short amount of time, all apparently from food poisoning from eating spaghetti at the Crowes' home.

Creamons laughs about it now, but he really thought he was going to die.

He played in the game, but the sudden weight loss had some impact on him.

THE BEST DEFENSIVE
TEAM IN AMERICA

John Kasay was convinced that Notre Dame had the best defensive football team in the United States of America.

"They had nine guys drafted from that defense," John recalled.

Their defense did jump out at you. It was quality through and through. Their defense was on par with the Nebraska defense we saw in the Sun Bowl in 1969. That was the year neither one of us should have been in El Paso, Texas. We were not good enough, and Nebraska was so good that it should have been in the Orange Bowl. They were there the next two years, winning back-to-back national championships.

The Pittsburgh defense in 1976, Texas in the 1983 Cotton Bowl—they were in that category. Over the 25 years I coached, the 1980 Notre Dame defense was one of the four or five best defenses that were in a class by themselves.

Their listed heights and weights were not too much out of the ordinary, but John learned from coaches who had played them that the listings were not accurate. Their players were bigger than advertised.

"I remember the day we practiced at Tulane when we were coming on the field as they were going off," Mike Fisher said. "We looked like a high school team."

"It was like we were going to play in the land of the giants," Tim Morrison echoed. "They were animals. But you know, once you hit them the first time, they are just regular guys."

"We knew they would be a good team," Chris Welton said. "And there was something about hearing the Notre Dame fight song in the Sugar Bowl. It is the fight song for about 50 percent of the world's high schools, but this time it was being played for Notre Dame."

"Notre Dame *was* college football," Lindsay Scott said. "And they were big. They were huge. My senior year in high school when I visited Clemson, I saw them play Notre Dame and they were the biggest people I had ever seen in my life. Those people were huge. They were bigger than we were. They were smarter. They had more prestige. In my mind I was thinking if it had to be anybody, why not Notre Dame?"

"They had one heck of a defense," Jim Blakewood said. "After playing them, I had even more respect for them. They were big, strong, and fast. We just couldn't do too much against them. It was not like we were giving Herschel any big holes to run through."

"No one expected us to win that game because Notre Dame was huge," Herschel Walker remembered. "They had all these big athletes. We were just a little country team from Georgia, but they didn't know what they had got a hold of."

"They were a who's who of college football," Robert Miles added. "We were from all these little-bitty places, and they were from Chicago and DeMatha and Moeller. We just wanted a shot at them."

In spite of how impressed he was with Notre Dame, John Kasay expressed great confidence that Georgia would win the game.

"They were real good, but they didn't have the same incentive that we had," John explained. "I was hoping Southern Cal would beat them so they would not have as much to play for."

John also got the impression from watching films that Notre Dame's players were so confident that they assumed they could play whenever they wanted to.

"Lots of times that bites you," John clarified. "You let it get too late or you discover that a team is better than you thought they were."

Southern Cal perhaps did us a favor by beating the Irish 20-3 in the season's last game.

BAD HISTORY IN NEW ORLEANS

This was not the first Georgia team that I had taken to the Sugar Bowl. The 1968 and the 1976 teams had gone, and both lost. The 1976 team was the one that ran into that great Pittsburgh defense and Heisman Trophy winner Tony Dorsett, too. They beat us 27-3.

The 1968 team lost to Arkansas 16-2.

"Everybody claims we were all out the night before the game," said Mike Cavan, starting quarterback on the 1968 team. "It wasn't true. I think Arkansas did a better job of getting ready to play.

"We all wanted to go to the Orange Bowl. We were hoping to play somebody higher ranked. We ended up going to Sugar Bowl, whatever the reason. Arkansas was the 10th-ranked team in the country. I don't think we gave them the proper respect. They looked upon it as an opportunity to play a great team that was ranked fourth in the country. We were looking at it from the other way. They played well, and we didn't."

MY FIRST TRIP TO NEW ORLEANS

Taking Georgia to the Sugar Bowl in 1968 was actually my second trip to the game. I made my first one in 1947.

As a boy I used to play football out in the street, and that was true on New Year's morning in 1947. My next-door neighbor, Mr. Tufi Leon, and his son, Francis, who used to play with me, were going to the Sugar Bowl. Mr. Leon asked me if I would like to ride over. He didn't have a ticket for me, but it sounded exciting.

I went in and talked to my daddy, and he gave me my yearly allowance of a dollar. So I thought I could get over there and get a ticket for a dollar. But once I got there, I heard a guy say he had two on the 50-yard line for $100. That was a lot of money back then.

But you have to remember that this was just before television, so tickets were big. This was a classic, too. It was Georgia with Charlie Trippi and North Carolina with Choo Choo Justice. Those were two players I had in my scrapbook. I really wanted to see those players.

I heard the roar of the crowd as the game started, and I was panicking because I didn't have a ticket. But I just watched the people file in, and I got more and more discouraged. I remember sitting on the curb by myself. I was hurt, but I was mad, too.

There was an old New Orleans cop who was standing there consoling me, and I remember telling him, "I tell you one thing! One of these days I am going to get into that place!"

Of course, the rest of the story is that not only did I get into the place, but I brought the first Georgia team that had been there since that day 22 years before. Of course, late in the fourth quarter, when it was obvious we were getting beat with about two minutes left, it is funny how your mind wanders. I thought to myself how much better off I was sitting out on the curb 22 years before.

No Curfew

I wanted the players to be involved in the game preparation for Notre Dame, so I got some of the seniors together and asked them to give me a recommendation on the curfew.

So they recommended no curfew the first night, 3 a.m. the second night and earlier and earlier until it was about 11 p.m. the night before the game. I was thinking, "What have I done?"

I had made a commitment, not to them but in my mind, that I wanted their recommendation and that I would basically accept it. I let them know I was concerned about it, but if I let them do this, they would commit to sticking to it. So I agreed.

I don't recall any problems. There is a misconception that Jim Blakewood missed the game after he cut his hand on a telephone cord. Someone told him that it was possible to yank a receiver off of a pay phone. He cut his hand when he tried it, but that was the next year against Pittsburgh.

Then we had to suspend Carnie Norris his senior season when we found him out in the hall at the hotel out of his mind before we played Penn State after the 1982 season. That was a case of something good coming from something bad. I sat down with him in my office when we got back to Athens and went down our roster, and he told me who was using drugs and who wasn't.

When this happened, none of us knew anything about drugs. The NFL at the time did not have a real drug program, except from an educational standpoint. However, they saw that it was something that they had to get into so they hired someone who was an expert. We got him to come down and spend three days with us.

He talked to the staff, and we could not believe what we were hearing. We even went to some drug rehabilitation places. He had some sessions with the team, and when he came back from that, he said that we had some problems that we needed to address.

We instituted the first drug education and drug-testing program in the country. Some schools had education, but nobody had testing. We started with football, and it grew from there. It was several years before the NCAA instituted a testing program. We were the first ones. We had people come from all over the country to talk to us because we were the model.

Years later I found out that Mike Fisher and Tim Bobo technically violated the curfew rules set by the team in 1980, but they were lucky. Mike's girlfriend, who later became his wife, showed up in New Orleans with some of her girlfriends, but they arrived in town one night before their room reservations.

They showed up at Fisher's door.

"Mike, we don't have any place to stay."

They knew if they got caught, they might get sent home, but they took the mattresses off the beds and made room for six girls in their room four nights before the national championship.

"Thank God we didn't get checked," Fisher laughed.

Yes, indeed, because Fisher had a key interception in the game.

So although you never completely relax with nearly a hundred young men in a town like New Orleans, the importance of the game was plenty of motivation to keep them focused.

Joe Creamons was among about eight Bulldogs who were down in the French Quarter when a dozen or so Notre Dame players came down the street. Our players invited their players to come inside and share a drink.

"Not only did they refuse, they totally ignored us," Creamons said. "They walked right by us."

DEDICATED TO THE LOYAL FANS

At a press conference before the game, I was asked who I would like to dedicate the game to, and I mentioned a fellow from Waycross, Georgia, named George Fesperman. He was the loyalist among loyalists. Back when alumni could be involved in recruiting, he had recruited John Donaldson to come to Georgia.

Regardless of what went wrong, George Fesperman was always supportive. In the darkest moments, he would write encouraging letters. He was a real gentleman and was humbly appreciative of my remarks that got a lot of play in the newspapers.

His grandson, Stuart Hunter Saussy, walked on and was our kicker in 1991. Mr. Fesperman is dead now, but he raised his family to be the same way, the most loyal of the loyal. He represented the loyal fans to whom the Notre Dame game was dedicated.

READY TO PLAY

Despite the natural distractions of a town like New Orleans, we were ready to play. I sensed it, and so did the coaches and players.

"I remember the special feeling on the field at New Orleans," said Bill Lewis. "All of a sudden, you realize what was about to take place, what was at stake. The enthusiasm and the anticipation were there to get ready to play the game."

"We were more focused because we knew the opportunity at hand," said Jeff Harper. "We knew the job we had to do. We also knew that this was not an opportunity that happens every day. This was a once-in-a-lifetime deal. We had a couple of nights out, but everybody realized we were getting ready for a ballgame. We came to play a game, not to take in the sights."

Harper was just an energetic guy. He was a go, go, go, go type. He would routinely get so excited that he would throw up before every practice and game.

"We knew we were ready to play a game when Jeff threw up," said Joe Happe. "The only time I ever threw up was before the Notre Dame game. I realized what we were about to do."

There is a story that Harper threw up on Scott Zedek, Notre Dame's big All-America tackle, early in the game. And that was the main reason Harper was able to handle Zedek throughout the game. We laughed about that for a long time.

A BAD START

Not only did Notre Dame drive for a field goal on their first possession, but Herschel Walker then got hurt on our second offensive play on a sweep out of bounds on the far side of the field. He came back to our sideline with his arm stuck up in the air. He didn't say anything, but that was Walker.

Hugh Nall (54) leads the Bulldogs onto the field at the Sugar Bowl.

"It was a toss sweep to the right," Walker recalled. "As I was going out of bounds, I got hit in the back, and it dislocated my shoulder. It was a weird feeling. The whole side of your body goes numb."

Some of the players didn't even know Walker had been hurt until after the game. His replacement, Carnie Norris, knew something was up when he went in the game so early. He was used to playing, but generally not so early.

I was busy, so I didn't know anything until Warren Morris, our head trainer, came up. The players and the coaches used to call him Dr. Death.

"Herschel is finished," Morris said. "He has dislocated his shoulder. He is finished for the game."

That was just what I wanted to hear. At first I was thinking, "Dr. Death, will you get out of here?" Then I thought, "What a way to start a game for the national championship."

While I was focused on the game, the trainers were telling Walker that he couldn't play. The word spread among the coaches and players on the sideline.

"That was a scary moment," Pat McShea said. "As he came out, you could tell he was in a lot of pain."

Mike Cavan told John Kasay, who felt his stomach flip.

"It was like eating a piece of soap," John said. "It was nauseating to hear."

"Butch Mulherin, the team doctor, couldn't find the dislocation at first," Mike recalled, "and for a fleeting moment I was thinking that maybe this game was bigger than Herschel might be."

"If it is dislocated, I want you to put it back," Walker told the trainers.

"Yeah, but that is going to hurt."

"It can't hurt any worse than it already does," he answered. "I didn't come all the way to New Orleans to play one or two plays."

So all this time I was thinking that we had to play the game without Walker. I made up my mind that was it. Then the next thing I knew, we had the ball back, and Walker went back in.

"They put his shoulder back in," Morris said. "He said he wanted to go."

So Walker returned and ran for 150 yards. No one had gone more than 100 yards all year against Notre Dame. That was how good their defense was. It would have been interesting to see what he might have done if he had not been hurt.

"It may have changed the way I ran," Walker added, "but I didn't think about it. I just did it."

"That is the essence of Herschel," Mike summed up. "He could play in a game of that magnitude with the injury he had and not worry about it. He wouldn't let his teammates down. He wouldn't do it."

TERRY HOAGE'S FIRST BIG PLAY

During the season, one of our freshmen, Terry Hoage, would occasionally block a field goal or an extra point in practice. He kept agitating and kept making his presence known, otherwise, I never would have thought about him. He was throwing his body around and blocking field goals, and he continued to do it day after day.

He was being red-shirted and was not scheduled to go to New Orleans, but he was practicing on the scout team against the varsity during bowl practice. That last week before Christmas, he kept blocking kicks. Just before our last tough practice at home before the Christmas break, Hoage did it again. He blocked a Rex Robinson field goal. That was when I sent him in from practice and told him to go pack. He was starting on our extra point and field goal blocking teams.

He played a critical role in turning the game around. We were down 3-0, Herschel Walker was hurt, and Notre Dame was lining up for another field goal. Only this time Hoage blocked it.

That was why he made the trip, because you knew one or two plays could make a difference. As it turned out, the next few plays in the game made all the difference.

Frank Ros remembered practicing with Hoage to perfect the block.

"I would get down in a nose guard stance and shoot through," he said. "Coach Russell had noticed that their kicker had a low trajectory, so he wanted me to go down on all fours and let the Freddie Gilbert jump off of me. Freddie had been a high-hurdler in high school."

Unfortunately, the design was better than the execution, because on the first attempt in practice, Gilbert kicked Ros in the fanny rather than jumping over him.

"I felt a sharp pain going up my ass," Ros recalled. "He caught me right in the cheek. Oww! Everybody was laughing, but I was in pain.

"Then Coach Russell asked Hoage to try, and he did exactly the same thing and kicked me in the ass."

Ros decided to switch tactics, shooting for the knees of his blockers, opening an avenue for Hoage to come through. And on Notre Dame's second field goal attempt, it worked, and Hoage blocked it. We got the ball in Notre Dame territory, and that set us up to drive for our own field goal.

Nobody knew who Terry Hoage was at the time. It was his only contribution all year, but when our whole secondary graduated the next year, he took advantage of the opportunity and became a starter, and then a two-time consensus All-American. He intercepted 12 passes in 1982, leading the nation, and in 1983 he was fifth in the Heisman balloting. He became one of the best defensive players we ever had and played 13 years in the NFL.

THE WORLD'S LONGEST ONSIDE KICK

We were a little more hopeful after Herschel Walker returned to the game on the field goal drive, so when we kicked off to Notre Dame after Rex Robinson's field goal, we felt like we were competitive again. But what followed was what many people have labeled the "world's longest onside kick."

I have heard it said that Archie Manning, who was the quarterback of the New Orleans Saints then, told us that there was a blind spot on kickoffs if you kicked the ball in a certain place in the Superdome. I have a vague recollection of something like that.

But really, the kickoff that turned the game looked like a miscommunication to me. It was one of those balls in the middle that looked like an "I got it, you take it" mixup. Kicking off from the 40, we usually tried to kick it in the end zone, and Robinson was able to do that so many times. So I don't think we intentionally tried to kick it to a hash mark.

"We used an old army tactic from the Civil War," Greg Bell said. "It's called a hinge move. The muscle guys would make a mess, and the hinge guys would come down and close them down. If you go back and look, we were pretty good on the kickoff."

The kick was between the two Notre Dame receivers, and neither one of them caught it. You never know how a football is going to bounce, particularly on Astroturf. And when it hit between the Notre Dame returners near the one-yard line, I think they were both stunned. Of course, everybody dived in after the ball.

The brothers from Savannah, Steve and Bob Kelly, charged in on the Notre Dame return man. Steve Kelly knocked the ball away, right before he dislocated his finger. And Bob Kelly was able to recover it. That set us up on the one-yard line in great position, and Walker dove in for our first touchdown.

THE PLAY OF A LIFETIME

A play like that sticks in your mind, and Bob Kelly remembers it vividly.

"Steve and I were side by side," he said. "I was the outside guy, and he was the inside guy. I ragged him all year about not hustling down, and it became a joke to see who could get down the field first."

Containment was Kelly's No. 1 priority. He had lost it only once all year, and that was at Auburn. Thank goodness for Freddie Gilbert's athleticism, or Auburn might have returned it all the way.

"When the ball hit on the Notre Dame one, it went straight up, like a great pitching iron shot," Kelly said. "I realized that the receivers for Notre Dame had screwed up pretty seriously. Steve went crashing in and kind of took out their first guy. The ball came flying out again, and I dove on it."

Greg Bell thought he was going to recover the ball.

"My eyes were bigger than a turnip," he said. "I never saw Bob, but he slipped right in there, and I fell on top of him. Steve made that play happen."

There was a melee at the bottom of the pile, but Kelly had a hammerlock on the ball. Kelly said he felt an adrenaline rush in the midst of the play. After the referee sorted out the pile and awarded him possession, his teammates picked him up.

"I still have the picture at home that *Sports Illustrated* sent me," Kelly said. "The ball is on the ground, Steve is on the ground, and I am diving for the ball. It was the flukiest play of my career, and the one I am best remembered for."

In the melee, one of Steve Kelly's fingers was dislocated and bent all the way back to his wrist.

"He was in so much pain he didn't care who had the ball," Kelly said. "In fact, when I got to the sideline, he wanted to know who got it. 'I did, brother.' Then they pulled that finger back in place."

"The Kelly boys were tough, tough football players," Bill Lewis said. "They were as tough a two as you ever want to coach. They fit the mold of the whole secondary that year: bright and eager to do anything to help the team. They could learn multiple positions."

To captain Frank Ros, the play epitomized the season.

"People always ask me what made that team unique, what was the one characteristic that stood out," Ros said. "It was that everybody gave 100 percent every time. The longest onside kick in the history of football is an example of that.

"If our guys are just running hard but not balls-out, that play never happens. The difference between Steve Kelly barely getting his hand where the guy was fixing to bring it in was literally a millisecond. If he had slowed down a little, if Bob Kelly is not running as hard as he can, it doesn't happen. Steve barely got his body on the ball. The Notre Dame guy was about to bring it in. It is a great example of where things happen when you are running hard. It is not always about great athleticism."

THE WEIRDEST PLAY EVER

Believe it or not, I actually remember a weirder kickoff. I was playing for Auburn, and we were down at Miami.

We kicked off, and as we did, the Miami front line turned their backs to run back to block. Well, it was a line-drive kick, and it hit one of their linemen in the rear, and it bounced right back to us. Fob James, my roommate, who later was governor of Alabama, caught it.

So Miami's front line is running back to block, and here we are, chasing them to block for Fob. The deep backs for Miami realized what had happened, and they were trying to tell the blockers to turn around. I think we gained about 30 yards before they figured out what had happened.

ANOTHER TURNOVER

We led the nation in takeaways that year, and we got another one to set up our second touchdown. Our captain, Frank Ros, made a big tackle, and Chris Welton recovered at the Notre Dame 22 to set up a short touchdown drive.

"It was basically a dive play," Ros recalled. "The hole opened up, and I stepped into the gut. He fumbled. The only reason I knew he fumbled was I heard, 'Oh my God!' in that Northern accent. I tried to spin off to find the ball, but Welton had it."

Ros considered the Notre Dame game the best one he ever played. Maybe it was because he was another Catholic who had followed the Irish as a child. He gave everything he had in that game.

"At the end of the game I was literally exhausted. I played the last three or four minutes with my shoulder pads undone."

Ros didn't realize how tired he was until after the game when he went out to eat with his family. He couldn't stop sweating.

Frank Ros reaches for a fumble by Notre Dame. He knew the ball was loose when he heard a Northern accent shout, "Oh my God!"

"I was miserable," he said. "Everybody else was having fun. I went back to the hotel and took a shower and walked down to Bourbon Street to a hot dog stand. But I was feeling so bad, I just walked back to the room."

ONE FOR SEVEN PASSING

We didn't complete but one pass against Notre Dame. I think that was just part of the great Notre Dame defense. They had some of the biggest defensive backs I have ever seen. They were all six foot three and 210 or 215 pounds. That is what you would like to have in a defensive back, and Notre Dame had them.

They would knock the heck out of our skinny receivers, just deck them. Plus they had a heck of a defensive line.

"I remember their secondary as young," Anthony Arnold said. "I thought it was one of their weak spots. A lot of the time we just didn't execute. We dropped a few passes."

"We dropped a touchdown pass going away," George Haffner agreed. "We had it set up and ran a post corner, and Buck Belue threw a beautiful ball. I thought that could have opened it up."

TIM CROWE'S BIG HIT

In the third quarter, Tim Crowe had one of the biggest hits I ever saw in a game. In my 25 years, it would go down as one of the biggest hits. It rattled the dome. The girders were bending after that one.

Crowe said I told him it was the biggest hit in Georgia football history. As far as I was concerned, it was. I don't remember one that was any louder or had a more stunning impact. Our defense was already playing well, but Crowe's tackle got us even more fired up.

"The play was a stunt," Crowe recalled. "I had John Scully, their center, in front of me. I was playing on his right shoulder, and I cut across on him. He missed me, and I had an almost direct shot at Phil Carter, their halfback. It was third down at the time, so this took them out of field-goal range. Coach Dooley always said it was the hardest hit he ever saw at Georgia."

"One More Time"

We were up 17-10, and Notre Dame just kept coming back down the field, time after time. Scott Woerner would always make a play. They kept throwing into the end zone, and any one of those balls could have been caught.

He intercepted one in the end zone and ran it out. I was giving him hell in my mind, but he got it out to about the 20 anyway. He had a terrific game. Herschel Walker was the game's MVP, but Woerner was runner-up.

We had to keep the ball at the end of the game. I did not want Notre Dame to get the ball another time. They had had too many opportunities, and we couldn't put the pressure on the defense again.

Erk Russell kept imploring the defense, "One more time." We said that often. Somehow, some way, one more time. We picked that up at midseason. That is the best kind of slogan, one that just happens.

It started with the South Carolina game as the momentum for the season began to build, and it became a real motivator. Before each game as the season headed toward a championship, the staff would remind the team, "Somehow, some way, one more time."

"Coach Russell must have said that about 10 times because we kept having to go out," Chris Welton recalled.

"Going into the fourth quarter, I started getting tired," Pat McShea said. "But that is one game you do not want to end where you are not fully spent. We fought for every inch."

"The speed of that game was unlike any I had ever played," Welton recalled. "Coach Russell used to talk about bodies flying through the air. In that game, they were. Nobody was going to leave anything on the field. It was emotionally draining, plus physically, we played a lot of plays."

"It was fast," Jeff Hipp agreed. "I don't remember sitting out any of that game."

"A lot of people forget you could smoke in stadiums back then," Welton added. "I remember a haze hanging over the field. Indoors. No breeze. Hot. I was soaking wet. I remember that last series, that I made a big tackle on second down."

Notre Dame's last thrust into the end zone was ended by another Woerner interception, set up by Woerner's swashbuckling style of play.

"In the Sugar Bowl, on the last series, Notre Dame ran a play on third down, a toss sweep," Welton said, "and I was in on the tackle just about on the line of scrimmage, and I look up and Scott is right

Defensive linemen Tim Crowe (91) and Joe Creamons celebrate the win over Notre Dame. Just before Christmas, Creamons went home with Crowe for the holidays fell sick with food poisoning. Creamons lost 14 pounds in two days and was still not at full strength for the game.

there with me. I had hit the guy inside, and Scott had hit him from the outside in.

"I said, 'What the hell are you doing? You have deep responsibility!' If they had thrown a halfback pass, the flanker would have been wide open.

"Scott said, 'Well, it just seemed like the thing to do.' The next play, their coaches had seen it. They faked the sweep and tried to throw the pass, and this time Scott is back with the receiver and makes the interception."

So we had to keep the ball, and that is why I was so ecstatic when we completed our one pass, from Buck Belue to Anthony Arnold, for seven yards. But even with that we still had to run the clock down.

I've seen a picture of Frank Ros and Mike Cavan coming up to congratulate me, and I am pointing at the clock. I was not ready to celebrate.

But then my expression changes, and I know we have it, and the celebration begins.

THE RED SEA

There was an explosion of fans on the field, a sea of red, as they say. I felt really bad that I couldn't find Dan Devine, the Notre Dame coach. We were swarmed. People were everywhere. It was great to see the excitement, but at the same time there is a tradition, a ritual, that you pay your respects to the other coach. This was his last game as a coach, too.

"I remember literally not being able to breathe," Chris Welton said. "People were all over you. I wanted to get away from that and go in the locker room."

Erk Russell had a box of cigars that he was going to pass out to his defensive players, but the swarm of fans dissuaded him.

"When those people started coming on the field, I knew we had to get out of there," Erk said. "It was almost an eerie setting with those people swarming the field."

"I was scared to death," Jim Blakewood said, "that I was going to fall and get trampled."

Fans were grabbing at the players, at their gear, trying to take away their helmets.

George Haffner, our offensive coordinator, was watching from the press box and saw his son picked up by one of the offensive linemen. He said the fact that Georgia had won the national championship first struck him when he heard it on the public address system as he was walking down to the locker room.

"I'll never forget that Cajun accent," George said. "'Congratulations to the University of Georgia. National champions.' That was when I felt a smile come across my face."

Someone picked Bob Kelly up and carried him around. He got a real bird-eye's view of the festivities.

Somebody ushered me over to television, but I wanted to get with the team. I remember running to the locker room, and I may have dived in. I'm not sure. But they picked me up and passed me around the room, up next to the ceiling. Not only did I feel like I was floating emotionally, I felt like I was floating physically.

I have been in a lot of joyous locker rooms, but there is nothing like winning it all, winning the championship. This was the national championship, and we had won them all—it was a joyous occasion.

Tim Morrison sat in front of his locker so tired that he could hardly find the energy to take his uniform off. Like many of the players, he had an excited family ready to go out and celebrate, but he just wanted to go home and go to bed.

I didn't want the night to end. Barbara noticed that I even compromised my discipline with the children, and they took advantage of it. Our youngest, Derek, 12 at the time, and his lifelong buddy, Hamp McWhorter—son of the late Boyd McWhorter, Georgia's dean and the SEC commissioner—ordered big thick porterhouse steaks from room service. That was something I would have never let them do, but that night it was fine.

I went up and down the hallways shaking hands and talking about the game. I do remember that night I never did take off my clothes. Barbara woke up the next morning, and I still had my sideline pass on, the same clothes, and, she said, a big smile on my face as I slept.

Chapter Fifteen

RETROSPECTIVE

Winning the national championship and all of the attention it garnered was exciting, but it also got to be distracting. It's a two-edged sword. You are too much in demand. How do you say no?

One of the nicest awards was the Gold Helmet Award as national coach of the year from the *Seattle Times* and the Seattle Seahawks. The people who give out these awards all want you to come out and be recognized, and they won't give it to you until you come. But there was no way that I could come on the prescribed date, because I had another scheduled engagement. Because we were the undisputed champions, they couldn't really give it to anyone else. For the first time ever, they let a player accept the trophy. Frank Ros, our captain, did the honors.

I do remember one particular banquet where I spoke after that season at Notre Dame, of all places.

After the swarm of fans in the Sugar Bowl prevented me from being able to speak to their coach, Dan Devine, I called him later and apologized. He appreciated the call.

In February, Father Joyce asked me to come up for at Dan's retirement dinner. I was the spokesman for the American Football Coaches Association.

Even though we had beaten them just a few weeks before, they were very gracious. Of course, they had been there before. I understood that the Notre Dame people were amazed at the reaction of the Georgia people, but I told them that if they had waited 89 years to win one, they would better understand it.

That was my first trip to the Notre Dame campus, the place I had dreamed of as a boy. It is an impressive campus. They have a beautiful chapel. Touchdown Jesus is a moving experience.

There is a bronze statue of the old athletic director Moose Krause. It's a bench, and he is sitting on it with a hat and a cigar in

Nat Hudson (far left), Frank Ros (center right), Jeff Hipp (far right), and I pose with the 1980 team's hardware.

his hand. He was a great basketball player up there, and everybody loved him. I remember many times he would punch me in the ribs and say, "Vince, you are one of us. You are one of us." He was talking about me being Catholic.

A few years later I did have a conversation with Father Joyce on a chance meeting on an airplane flight. Father Joyce was the executive president of Notre Dame University and the most respected administrator in college athletics at the time. We visited about how Notre Dame was looking for a head coach, and he wanted to start a discussion with me if I had any interest. I told him if he had asked me 15 years earlier, I would have come right away. But I had been at Georgia too long.

THE ULTIMATE ACHIEVEMENT

Winning the national championship is the ultimate achievement for a college football coach. It is really the culmination, what you play for, what you aspire to. To have a team that wins them all and is named the national championship really is the ultimate. That is what it is all about. It is why you compete. The goal is to have your team declared the undisputed No. 1 team in the country, without question, and that 1980 team did it and reached that ultimate goal.

It was the seed for the next four years. That 1980 team really developed an attitude that we were going to find a way to win. Each and every game, somebody in some phase of the game had to step forward. Every phase of the game would have its moment.

You could break it down into the three big components—offense, defense, and special teams, but you could also look at the parts of each component. If the running game was struggling, you have to be able to pass. If the passing game was struggling, you had to be able to run. Somebody has to step up and do something.

We used to always say that there are about 165-plus plays on average in a game, but when you get down to it, there are three or four plays that will make a difference. But you never know when those three or four plays will come. It might be on the first play of the game, or it might be the last play of the game. You have to play every play like this play could be the one or two or three or four plays that make a difference in the game.

For the most part, the 1980 team did that. We had a team that played hard and fought hard every play.

I've never really thought too much about what might have happened if we had not had those key plays here and there in 1980 that enabled us to win the championship. There were other years where we didn't win, for example, in 1982. What if Penn State had dropped the pass they caught late in the game?

But I will say this, if it had not happened, there would have been a void in my career. To have coached 25 years and never felt the ultimate would have left me somewhat unfulfilled.

We played Arkansas three times in bowl games and lost to them the first two times, 16-2 in the 1969 Sugar Bowl and 31-10 in the 1976 Cotton Bowl. I said to myself, I don't think I ever want to retire until we beat Arkansas in a bowl game. We finally beat them 20-17 in the 1987 Liberty Bowl when John Kasay, the son of John Sr., kicked a field goal on the last play of the game.

That was something because as I looked back on my career, I'm not sure if we had lost to Arkansas if I would have retired, because I would not have been totally fulfilled.

Although I had thought about retiring on occasion, I did not fully make up my mind to do so until the end of the 1988 regular season. It was my 25th year. I made the decision because I had done everything that I ever really wanted to do. There was nothing left. I was fortunate to be able to achieve that.

But if we had not won the national championship and if we had not beaten Arkansas, I am not sure I would have retired.

I have been an athletic director who has observed many of our teams win that ultimate national championship. We've won team

Georgia fans celebrate the Sugar Bowl win, an undefeated season, and a national championship. *Photo by Frank Fortune*

championships in men's and women's tennis and golf, gymnastics, women's swimming, and baseball. You can feel a part of those experiences in different ways.

It is a great thrill to be watching the men's tennis team win at 3:30 a.m. during the NCAA championships here in Athens, cheering every point. It is scintillating to be out in California and watch the women's team beat Stanford and win the national championship. I was ecstatic to be with Jack Bauerle when his women's swimming teams won three straight national titles. I'll never forget our men's and women's golf teams walking off the green as national champions. Being in Omaha when the baseball team won its first

College World Series was a thrill. I witnessed all five of the titles won by our gymnastics team. Our most recent sport, equestrian, has ridden to two national championships. Winning it all is an absolutely great feeling.

But if I had not experienced being a coach of a national championship team myself, then I wouldn't quite know how special it is.

All of the teams I coached were special to me. Asking which one is my favorite is like asking me which one of my children I love the best. Some of our teams that struggled may have accomplished as much as they could have with what they had. Every team was special in that regard.

But the 1980 team has that distinction because they won the national championship. You can't take that away from them. That will always separate them from all the rest.

AFTERWORD

Did Georgia win the national championship because the team was close, or was it close because it won the national championship?

The short answer is yes.

When you talk to the players who made up that team, the almost universal theme is how tight knit that 1980 team was.

"It is my fondest memory of playing football," said Herschel Walker, who certainly played more football than any other lettermen from the 1980 team. "We were taught teamwork. That season is the greatest example of teamwork. We didn't have all the great superstars."

To most observers, Walker himself was the superstar. But to his credit, he was viewed by his teammates as just that, a teammate.

But Walker himself was also quick to credit those players paving the way with their blocks. When he went to New York for the Heisman Trophy banquet, he took along Chris McCarthy, a sophomore fullback in 1980 who followed the tradition set by Jimmy Womack and Ronnie Stewart.

"People always say, 'Herschel, you did this, you did that,'" Walker said. "No. It was the offensive line. I had the best offensive line in football. I didn't get hit in the backfield. I got hit down the field. That is the sign of a good offensive line."

Walker even goes so far as to suggest that another running back could have enjoyed just as much success running behind the likes of Wayne Radloff, Joe Happe, Hugh Nall, Jim Blakewood, Tim Morrison, Jeff Harper, Warren Gray, and Nat Hudson.

"Herschel came in as humble as they come," said Marty Ballard, whose role in 1980 was that of a player-coach. "He fit right in with us. There were no prima donnas on that team. Really, we were short on talent and big on guts."

Hudson said the 1980 team was like a first-aid kit.

"We had whatever we needed for whatever ailed us," he said.

"We were a group of guys who pulled together and had a common goal," Morrison explained.

"It was a great experience," said Hugh Nall, who stayed in football as a coach. "I learned never to say never. The biggest thing that came through was the camaraderie. The longer I have been in the business now, and I look back at the championship teams I have been involved in as a coach, they are always different and a little bit special, but I have never felt one like we had that year. I think the biggest thing is I think we just had a lot of good kids."

"We had a big group of seniors who had a lot of character," posited Frank Ros, the team captain. "I calculated one time that 17 got degrees. Five of those got masters degrees and one got a law degree."

Many still wear their rings. Anthony Arnold never wore his ring. He gave it to his father in appreciation for his support through the years.

But even without the rings, their names are recognized.

"I am the last person to tell someone I played football," Jeff Harper said. "I don't use that as a way to get in the door, but once people find out, that is all they want to talk about. Playing for Georgia changed my life."

They all have stories of being "found out."

"You are suddenly a celebrity," Chris Welton stated. "All of a sudden, you are a big man in that environment. It even makes my kids proud."

Doors to profitable ventures have opened to lettermen for Georgia's 1980 national champions just by virtue of name recognition. But what the former players truly seem to treasure is the close companionship they have maintained with their teammates.

"I enjoyed my days at Georgia," Harper confessed, "and to this day they are still some of my fondest memories and some of my closest friends."

"Scott Woerner and I talk about every other day," Welton said.

Ros has carried on as captain of the team, organizing reunions and trying to help the team members stay in touch with each other.

When Jimmy Payne was diagnosed with cancer, Georgia lettermen started a fund to help with his expenses. Tragically, the disease claimed Payne so quickly that tens of thousands of dollars remained in the fund. The lettermen named the fund in his honor and today dispense the money to other Georgia players in need.

Tim Crowe personally saw how his teammates would respond when his home burned down. Checks started showing up at his house, some with a little good-natured teasing. Crowe is a fireman.

It was not a perfect group. Some struggled in life. Carnie Norris served time. Lindsay Scott wasted a fortune, a football career, and a family because of drugs. A few have yet to get that degree.

"Life has brought me down to earth," Scott said. "That is the truth."

But just as he made a comeback from troubles during the climactic 1980 season, Scott has come back in life, too.

"I appreciate those times at Georgia," he said. "As you get older, you learn to appreciate those times and cherish those times. None of that is guaranteed. You don't do any of it by yourself. A lot of times, pride and ego says I can do it by myself. But certain situations call for raising your hand and saying I need some help."

They also have grown to appreciate their coach, Vince Dooley.

"He gained the respect of the players," John Kasay said. "Then they didn't like him, because he held them to a high standard. After they left and saw how unfair the world is they learned, this guy taught us something."

"Coach Dooley was very authoritative, a disciplinarian even," Jim Blakewood said. "When I was younger, I was scared of him."

Blakewood was impressed that Dooley agreed to help underwrite Blakewood's pursuit of his degree after his eligibility expired.

"He didn't bat an eye," Blakewood said. "He told me that as long as I was making satisfactory progress, he would pay for it.

"I was very close to my father. Eight years after I played, my father passed away. Coach Dooley made a personal call to my home. I don't know if the rest of the athletic directors in the country would have done that. It just showed that he cared about me. He cared about his players."

John Kasay played on Dooley's first teams and coached many years for Dooley. His son grew up a Bulldog and kicked for Georgia.

"I thought he was a hell of a football coach," John said. "There are two things he taught me that I will always thank him for. The first was the ability to be discreet, to think about what you are going to do first before you do it. Give yourself enough time to make a good decision. You cannot remember a time where you heard him say something about someone or did something that you were ashamed of.

"The other thing was he always talked about having a plan. He didn't like going out on the field and shooting from the hip."

The plan never came together like it did in 1980.

"We won a national championship because we believed in each other," Walker said.

"For all practical purposes, based on what was on paper, we had no business winning the national championship," Ros said. "We were part of something that never should have happened at the University of Georgia."

But it did.

—BLAKE GILES

The 1980 Georgia Bulldog National Championship Team